PROTEIN POW

ALSO BY ANNA SWARD

The Ultimate Protein Powder Cookbook

PROTEIN POW

QUICK AND EASY
PROTEIN POWDER RECIPES

GLUTEN-FREE, SOY-FREE, HEALTHY SNACKS

PROTEIN
POW

ANNA SWARD

THE COUNTRYMAN PRESS
A DIVISION OF W. W. NORTON & COMPANY
Independent Publishers Since 1923

For information about permission to reproduce selections from this book, write to
Permissions, The Countryman Press, 500 Fifth Avenue, New York, NY 10110

For information about special discounts for bulk purchases, please contact
W. W. Norton Special Sales at specialsales@wwnorton.com or 800-233-4830

Manufacturing by RR Donnelley, Shenzhen
Book design by Faceout Studio, Paul Nielsen
Production manager: Devon Zahn

The Countryman Press
www.countrymanpress.com

A division of W. W. Norton & Company, Inc.
500 Fifth Avenue, New York, NY 10110
www.wwnorton.com

978-1-58157-464-7 (pbk.)

10 9 8 7 6 5 4 3 2 1

TO ZOE:

The Absolute Love of My Life

CONTENTS

Introduction 9

Protein 101 13

Using This Cookbook 23

PROTEIN BARS 30

PROTEIN TRUFFLES 66

PROTEIN CHOCOLATE CUPS 108

PROTEIN PANCAKES 122

PROTEIN MUG CAKES 162

Acknowledgments 195

Index 197

INTRODUCTION

Making your own healthy protein-based snacks is extremely quick and easy. It's the kind of thing that, once you try, you find yourself doing every week, sometimes even every day. I've been making my own protein foods—bars, truffles, pancakes, cakes, pizzas ... you name it—for over ten years now. I started off like most people do: with protein shakes. I was in college, regularly running and training at the gym several times a week, so I bought a tub of protein to fortify my diet. I did exactly what the label told me: I added two scoops to a shaker with water, shook it, and downed it. Before long, though, I got bored. I mean, don't get me wrong, a protein shake is nice every now and then. It's basically a nutritious milkshake and who doesn't love milkshakes, right? But I got bored with them quickly and, alongside my boredom, there was something else I didn't like: the fact that I was drinking a bunch of protein and calories in a matter of minutes (sometimes seconds!) and that was it. And I'd rather eat than drink my calories. It's more fun that way, you know? More satisfying. So I stopped drinking shakes and, instead, started adding protein to my oatmeal. I started making cookies with it. I started making cakes, pizza, bread, muffins, even donuts! The more I used protein powder in my foods, alongside other nutrition-dense ingredients—such as fruits, veggies, nuts, and seeds—the more I realized that using protein powder as an ingredient in snacks and healthy meals was a revolution waiting to happen.

I started doing all this back in 2010, back when protein powder-based recipes only existed in obscure bodybuilding forums that contained low-res food photos that looked as if they came straight out of a horror film—you know, gray foods, amorphous cakes, shiny abominations that didn't look appetizing in the slightest. It was either that or the recipes showed no photos at all. You had no idea what you were getting into. On the Internet back then, there was very little guidance, help, or advice on how to cook with protein powders. Traditional chefs rejected them, viewing protein powders in general as "fake food." Foodies weren't touching protein powders of any kind either. Most people simply didn't regard or approach protein powders as they would food. They saw them as muscle-building supplements, not as something they could or would want to cook with. Plant-based protein powders were especially foreign to most people. When they were released into the mainstream market, around 2010, nothing was being written about using, let alone cooking with, veggie protein powders at all. No one knew what to do with them. To the vast majority of people, protein powder equaled whey protein, and whey protein equaled shakes. That's where the conversation began and ended. So when veggie protein powders came out, people had no idea what to expect. The ones who tried them, immediately approached them as they would whey—they'd throw a scoop in their blender and POW! Expect a shake. But they were quickly disappointed because, unlike whey protein, plant-based protein powders don't really yield thick and "milkshakey" shakes—they're more savory, thicker, and far less creamy. As a result, most people cast veggie protein powders aside.

So I taught myself. I went through a lot of trial and error to better understand how to cook not just with whey protein, but with all the other protein powders that slowly emerged as the years went by. I became a mad scientist of sorts, turning my kitchen upside down every time I got back from the gym, feeding my family all sorts of "experiments." And I learned a lot! I learned that protein powder should never be treated as white flour and that you should never substitute whey protein with a plant-based protein. I learned that, for best results, you should try to make sure your batter is made up of less than 30 percent whey protein when baking, otherwise your food will end up hard and rubbery. I learned how to read ingredient labels and that, as alluring as flavored and pre-sweetened proteins can be, unflavored products give you the freedom to flavor and sweeten your foods however you like. I learned that protein powder is not a muscle-growing magic potion—it's just food, like eggs are just food, like chicken.

Through proteinpow.com, I journaled my protein-cooking experiments over the years and built a global community of followers whose excitement and engagement began to cause a ripple effect. Thanks to our burgeoning community, the popularity of our Protein Pow app, and the rise of my previous cookbook, *The Ultimate Protein Powder Cookbook*, we played a major role in turning cooking with protein powder into a movement, that, today, transcends borders and unites people worldwide. We grabbed it from the shadows and thrust it into the limelight so that, today, if you go to any healthy-eating café or restaurant, you'll probably find protein pancakes or protein energy balls on their menu.

Today, using protein powder has gone mainstream. If you open any fitness and nutrition book or magazine, chances are high you'll run into a protein powder–based recipe. Your favorite celebrities? Yeah, most of them use protein powders every day. So do athletes, as do many busy professionals, moms, dads, and even grandparents across the world. If you Google or search for "protein recipes" or #ProteinRecipes on Facebook or Instagram, you'll find hundreds of thousands of posts; posts from people all over the world who, instead of using their protein powders for shakes, have chosen to make delicious foods with them. They're posts from people from all walks of life who choose to think outside the shake! After reading this book, I bet you'll be joining in the ranks too, hashtagging #ProteinRecipes and #ProteinPow with gusto—sharing your recipes, snacks, and journeys through this oh-so-exciting brand-new world of protein **POW!** Because why have a shake when you can have cake?

PROTEIN 101

Protein is a key nutrient and is essential to our health. It comprises amino acids—our body's building blocks—and it repairs, maintains, and builds muscle and connective tissue. Besides water, protein is the most abundant organic compound in our body: it's found in our hair, skin, muscle, and connective tissue. Every part of our body is made up of protein. Without protein, we wouldn't be able to function! We'd experience weakness, fatigue, hair loss, muscle loss, and eventually . . . we'd give up the ghost.

You can find varying amounts of protein in meat, fish, chicken, dairy, pulses, and beans. Many fruits and vegetables contain protein too, but only in small amounts. This means that, in the course of your daily food intake, you consume protein. But do you consume enough? And, more important, do you pay attention to where that protein comes from, and what else you are getting alongside protein in your food?

If you exercise regularly, have an active job, and/or lead an active lifestyle that involves being on your feet throughout much of the day, you can benefit from incorporating protein into your meals and snacks. That's because, in addition to making you feel fuller for longer, protein-containing foods (compared to high-sugar foods) can help you stabilize your energy and focus by balancing your blood sugar levels. That means greater satiety and reduced carb/sugar cravings. In addition to making you feel, function, and perform your very best, eating nutrient-dense foods as well as protein is key when it comes to losing fat while maintaining (or even gaining) muscle tissue. Remember: protein builds muscle and the more lean muscle mass your body has, the more efficient it is at burning fat.

Now, you may have heard people say that, as a population, we're already eating enough protein; that there's no point in having more; that protein powders are pointless or only suitable for bodybuilders or elite athletes. Personally, I disagree with those kinds of blanket statements for a number of reasons. First, there is not a set amount of protein that everyone needs. Protein requirements are different for each person and depend on a number of factors: a person's age, gender, size, activity level, occupation, and medical history. Not everyone requires the same amount of protein, so giving a blanket figure is irresponsible, in my opinion, because it gives people the impression that they don't need to conduct further research into what's right for them specifically; it gives them the impression they don't need to find out more. When they absolutely do! Everyone should strive to find out what kind of diet they respond to and feel best with; what kind of macronutrient split (i.e., what ratio of carbs to protein and fat) works best for them. We're not all gingerbread people at the end of the day, cut out of the same dough. We're complicated machines that require more careful calibration.

There are various public guidelines released by health organizations that you can and should consult to get started. But bear in mind that they're guidelines, not strict directives, and it's important to go beyond guidelines when it comes to assessing how many calories and how much protein, fat, and carbs, your body needs and responds best to. A quick consultation with a certified nutritionist can do a lot to get you closer to a more accurate answer, but, above all, listen to your own body.

Second, macronutrients—grams of protein, carbs, and fat—aren't all we should be focusing on. Doing so disregards the fact that micronutrients (vitamins, minerals) matter just as much to our health and we should be paying attention to them too.

When it comes to diet in general, and protein in particular, listen to your body and do your best to consume nutrition-dense foods as often as you can. You don't need to count every calorie, every macro, and micro-manage your diet if you don't want to. Just eat in a way that makes you feel good and allows your body to perform optimally. Don't just look at the grams of protein you're consuming without at the same time looking at where that protein is coming from and what else is coming with it. Don't buy into sensationalist drivel or cookie-cutter programs, fads, and unsustainably restrictive diets that promise you the world. Listen to your body, first and foremost, and spend a bit of time looking into what works best for you.

The recipes in this cookbook show you how healthy and delicious snacking can be when your snacks are jam-packed with not only protein but also other all-natural healthy ingredients. Everything here is a tribute to the fact that you can satisfy your sweet tooth and cravings without diving into a sugar bowl or eating foods packed with artificial sweeteners, soy, fillers, cane sugar, artificial colors, artificial flavors, preservatives, bulk ingredients, additives, and other junk. The recipes in this cookbook all contain a nutritional breakdown, including kcals (calories), grams of protein, grams of carbohydrates, and grams of fat. Go ahead and record these nutritional breakdowns in your food diary, if you track your macronutrients for personal or health reasons. If you don't track your macronutrients, still check out the nutritional breakdown of each recipe if you want to better understand what makes up the foods in this cookbook.

Ultimately, the recipes here are a step toward empowering you to make your own snacks, always knowing exactly what goes into your food. They're all extremely easy. You don't need to have any special cooking skills to make the recipes in this book—they're all quick, simple, and almost impossible to get wrong. They're also adaptable to different nutritional needs. So, for example, if a recipe you see is too high in carbohydrates because it uses coconut sugar, honey, date syrup, or agave, you can tweak it by using a lower-calorie and lower-sugar sweetener. You can also bump up the protein content in any snack by simply adding more protein powder! It's really that easy. Just approach your cooking with confidence, be willing to experiment, and have fun!

PROTEIN POWDERS:
NOT JUST FOR ATHLETES

Most protein powders and protein-based products are marketed to a super-fit and young audience. For example, if you look at the way in which many protein supplements are advertised, you'll see bulging muscles everywhere, oiled physiques, and youthful, "perfect" bodies. You won't find many protein powders with a fifty-plus person on the label—you probably won't find a single wrinkle or un-Photoshopped body in sight. That kind of imagery simply isn't regarded as "sexy" to mainstream protein companies, you know? It doesn't sell widely, at least not to a general population intent on chasing a kind of flawless and indestructible forever-young look. Of course, that's not to say that older people aren't targeted with protein-containing products. They sometimes are. There are products out there—drinks, primarily—that are aimed at a senior market, often in a medical setting, in order to calorically boost someone's diet. Usually, however, most of these products tend to be curative instead of preventative. They're prescribed to people whose intake of protein is dangerously low.

Ensuring a sufficient intake of nutrients and protein, as well as engaging in some form of cardiovascular and resistance training, is key to preventing (and in many cases, treating) sarcopenia, i.e., age-related muscle loss. Yet it's not something that you see protein companies screaming about. Probably because, again, it's not as sexy as having a bikini-clad model or an oiled, muscular man on a label or billboard. The mainstream conceptualization of protein as a product for only young and athletic people however, overlooks the fact that protein has a huge impact and it is extremely important for all of us, particularly as we age. So why not incorporate protein more as an ingredient in our diet as opposed to perceive it as simply a muscle-building supplement?

CHOOSING A PROTEIN POWDER

Unlike my previous cookbook, which uses flavored proteins of all kinds (whey, casein, pea, hemp, rice, beef, and egg), this cookbook uses only three: whey protein, pea protein, and hemp protein. All of the proteins I used are single-ingredient proteins with absolutely nothing added: not even soy or sunflower lecithin. They are single-ingredient proteins: rBGH-free whey and non-GMO pea and hemp protein powders. The reason for this is simple.

I've been cooking with protein powders for many years now and sharing my recipes at proteinpow.com, on the Protein Pow app, and in cookbooks. One of the biggest things I've noticed people have an issue with, when it comes to successfully following protein powder-based recipes (whether mine or anybody else's), is finding a protein powder that translates from the author's recipe to the food they make at home. So, let's say someone posts a recipe for vanilla whey protein pancakes and someone else goes on and makes it. That first person may actually have been using a whey protein that has a lot of added gums (like guar gum, xanthan gum, etc.), sweeteners, and flavorings. That second person may use a protein powder with no added gums but with a lot of fillers instead, such as soy protein or wheat protein. Even though those two people may have been using a tub labeled as "vanilla whey protein powder," the final product they each make will be widely different! That's why, in all the recipes in this book, I've used plain protein powders, with absolutely nothing added in. I've done it also because, the more I've learned about this industry, the more I've realized that we simply don't need any of the extra stuff most companies add to their protein powders. We don't need any artificial sweeteners and artificial flavors. We don't need any hydrogenated oils or low-quality sources of protein. We don't need a lot of the ingredients that companies add to their powders in order to give them a better, more "milkshakey" mouth-feel when shaken with water. When it comes to food—like protein bars, truffles, pancakes, or mug cakes—you don't need those ingredients at all. In fact, having them in your protein powder can work against you! Gums, for instance, can become toothpaste-y when heated, contributing to a rubbery mouthfeel and dry texture. And some artificial sweeteners and artificial flavors are, well, frankly nasty. Why use a "chocolate" protein powder that features no chocolate at all when you can use real cocoa powder, you know? Which on top of tasting delicious, packs antioxidants and is really good for you, too.

PROTEIN POWDERS

If you regularly buy and consume protein powder, chances are you've met someone who has told you that protein powders are unnatural, as bad as any other processed food, and/or "not real food." You know, people who skeptically regard protein powders as strange concoctions designed for bodybuilders (men) to quickly gain muscle mass. I know, I've met a lot of them! More than I can count by now. Something that they seldom acknowledge, though, is the fact that protein powder—whey protein powder, in particular—is part of A LOT of FOODS they wouldn't categorize as "not real."

LET'S START WITH WHEY PROTEIN: Did you know that most baby formula contains whey protein powder? Yup. Pretty much all baby

formula does, except of course the dairy-free varieties for lactose-intolerant babes. Most baby formulas contain whey isolate and/or concentrate, the same stuff that is commonly sold as a food supplement or ingredient to you and me. Baby formula contains the same stuff that we purchase in a tub, only theirs goes through extra tests and quality control measures: it is micro-analyzed and, when necessary, micro-filtered further in order to create a purified product that does not impact the delicate immune system of infants. Whey protein is used in baby formula because of its unique nutritional benefits as well as its ability to deliver all the essential amino acids required for optimal growth and development in babies who are unable to drink breast milk. It's a nutrition powerhouse!

The whey protein in baby formula is the same product we grown-ups commonly purchase in tubs: it's the byproduct of the manufacture of cheese; it's a nutrient-dense food derived from milk which most people at least deem suitable for human consumption. It's food, real food.

As mentioned in the previous section, whey protein is regularly found in nutritive drinks aimed to tackle malnutrition, age-related muscle loss, blood glucose control, and weight management. But did you know that a lot of the packaged food that we regularly buy contains whey protein too? Breads, pizza bases, yogurts, cookies, confectionery, hot chocolate, sauces, salad dressings, processed meats, an assortment of flavored drinks . . . you name it! Whey (as well as other plant-based protein powders like pea protein) is a valuable nutrition-rich ingredient used in foods designed to be consumed by people of all ages.

Unfortunately, however, marketing campaigns continue to paint protein powder as some kind of muscle-building magic dust, to such a degree that the general population regards whey protein powder supplements with skepticism. Women, especially, think of protein powder as some kind of gender-exclusive muscle potion. This explains why there are so many women-only powders designed to be white and pink, with labels including words such as "toning," "weight loss," and "diet" in order to assuage what marketers perceive to be women's fear of mass and muscle-gain. This kind of advertising, however, is deceptive at best and harmful at worst, because it misconstrues the fact that protein powder is food. It's not magic. It shouldn't be exclusively regarded as a supplement, not when it can be approached and used as a nutritious ingredient to make healthy meals and snacks.

Now, don't get me wrong: A LOT of protein powders out there

are filled with enough junk that the "real food" description and label doesn't apply to them. I'm talking about powders with a ton of extra ingredients, from artificial flavors, colors, and sweeteners to fillers, gums, genetically modified ingredients, corn syrups, and a huge array of hydrogenated oil and cheap corn derivates. The ingredient lists of many powders out there are long and can read like science projects! If you must, go ahead and label those powders as "not real food." Go ahead and avoid them.

But don't bunch together all plain protein powders into the same category as the randomness-filled tubs of powder sold to muscle-bound Adonises. Plain protein powders—the kind with nothing added in—can be a wonderful addition to anyone's pantry.

VEGGIE PROTEINS, including pea, hemp, and rice protein powder, are much like whey, in that they are added to a lot of commercially available foods to enhance their nutritional profile. These foods are consumed by people of all ages, from kids to older folks alike. Veggie protein powders are regularly (and increasingly) added to cereals, breads, pizza bases, and vegan products because they're wonderful thickeners and nutritive ingredients. As you'll notice in this book, my previous one, and all the recipes I've published at proteinpow.com, pea protein powder has a lot of applications. That's why I cook with it so much! It's a great ingredient to incorporate into one's diet.

To sum up, protein powders, in their plain form, really are just food. And they can be included in everyone's diet as a low-calorie, nutrition-dense ingredient. As long as you read your ingredient labels and buy protein powders that don't feature a whole ton of pointless junk, you really are buying food. Protein powder shouldn't be feared or approached with mistrust. Just choose one or two tubs of one-ingredient protein powders and **POW!** A whole world of healthy deliciousness will unfold before you.

PROTEIN POWDERS AND SUSTAINABILITY

In addition to being convenient, versatile, and packed full of goodness, protein powders should also be considered in the context of sustainability—as environmentally-friendly substitutes for meat. That is, in my opinion, one of the most important reasons why we ought to not only demystify but also promote protein powders' mainstream consumption. Hear me out:

Protein powders are a fantastic option for people who want to diversify their intake of protein and move away from relying solely on poultry, fish, and livestock sources. We're running out of farmable land and (potable) water, all the while greenhouse gas emissions are at an all-time high. Turning to alternative sources of protein is, in my view, extremely important!

This is actually a huge (though often unvoiced) reason why I love buying, cooking with, and consuming protein powders such as whey and other veggie sources: because they're a byproduct of the creation of something else. They're something that, if we don't eat it, will get discarded. Whey, for example, is a byproduct of cheese production, just like hemp protein is a byproduct of the extraction of oil from hemp seeds. Pea and rice protein are less of a byproduct of the creation of something else but their manufacture is not as problematic as the (industrial) farming of animals for protein. Protein powders can be an excellent source of protein for vegetarians, vegans, and pretty much everyone!

WOMEN'S PROTEIN POWDERS

I always tell my readers and Protein Pow fans to stay away from women-only protein powders. Those products (usually sold in big pink tubs with "toning" slapped on the label) depict a misleading picture about what women's nutrition should be like. In truth, a woman's diet should be much like a man's! Only, well . . . we need less overall food because, as a product of our size, musculature, and hormones, (most) women burn fewer overall calories than (most) men. Women don't need any special foods. You don't see "women-only" chicken out there, so why protein powder? Women also don't need soy which, for some reason, is heavily marketed to them. Soy is a cheap source of protein that I always advise women to steer away from. Women most certainly don't need special protein designed to tone them, either. It's the same with exercise. Far too many products, publications, and even exercise programs out there support the idea that women should somehow train differently from men; otherwise they'll get "bulky." But that's not true! Women can (and I think should!) lift heavy weights, follow a regular diet, and include gender-neutral (i.e., NORMAL) protein in their day-to-day lives, without transforming into female versions of the Hulk. It's physically impossible! The reality is that women who strength-train and eat well (and enough) usually end up feeling better, performing better, and looking better too!

TOP THREE REASONS TO MAKE YOUR OWN PROTEIN SNACKS

Quality

When you make your own snacks, you have control over what goes into them. No endless list of ingredients. No cheap fillers like soy, corn, and wheat protein. No hydrogenated fats, palm oils, gums, humectants, artificial sweeteners, artificial flavors, etc. When you make your own snacks, all you need are a handful of nutrition-dense ingredients and presto! Nutrition-packed deliciousness at your fingertips.

Freshness

Homemade protein bars and truffles are a great and fresh alternative to ready-made snacks found on store shelves. Unlike commercially made snacks that regularly include preservatives and shelf-life–extending additives, the foods you make at home aren't designed to last on the shelf for all eternity. They're fresh, every time.

Customized Perfection

When you make your own snacks, you can tweak their ingredients to match your taste and dietary preferences, your macronutrient needs, and your appetite. If you love all chocolate things like I do, then add a ton of cocoa to your bars! Like the orange-chocolate combo? Make some chocolate bars and zest a bit of an orange into your batter (see page 60). Want lower-carb bars? Use a naturally low-carb sweetener such as granulated stevia. Want your snacks to be lower in calories and fat? Reduce the amount of nut butters and chocolate you use. Want a smaller snack? Make bite-sized bars or truffles. Want your snacks to be vegan? Use a plant-based protein powder instead of whey—just remember, you will always need a bit more milk and "flour" when substituting pea protein for whey. Want to be 100 percent certain that your bars are gluten-free? Use only certified gluten-free ingredients. The sky's the limit to what you can do!

When you make your own snacks, they're much tastier than anything found on the shelf! No hardness or difficult-to-chew textures. No snacks that are too sweet for you, or not sweet enough. When you make your own, you end up with customized perfection, every time!

Making your own snacks is not only easy and quick, it's also a lot of fun! Invite your whole family to be part of the process. All the recipes for bars (see page 30), truffles (see page 66), and cups (see page 108) are no-bake, so they don't require an oven or microwave.

SHOPPING GUIDE

Buying Protein: Always Read the Label

When you go out and choose a protein powder, protein food, or protein drink, I urge you to always select the simplest option available. I made all the recipes in this book using a simple one-ingredient, high-quality protein powder—nothing else added to it, not even lecithin. I recommend you go down this route too. Try to avoid products that contain soy, a heap-ton of artificial ingredients, and cheap bulk ingredients. A lot of proteins don't explicitly mention all their ingredients, so remember to always turn tubs over, put your monocle on, and read ingredient labels. I say this because you may be buying a protein powder marketed as whey, casein, pea, hemp, or rice protein only to find out by reading its ingredient label that its second or third ingredient is soy protein and that it contains a bunch of nutrition-void ingredients. The same goes for protein bars and protein foods. Forget the way products are marketed and pay attention to ingredient labels instead. Always let them do the talking.

Know Your Proteins

Avoid "premium" brands that don't mention soy, wheat, or a bunch of other artificial and bulk ingredients in their description yet feature them as primary ingredients. Why? Because the inclusion of these products compromises the overall quality of the protein powder you are buying. These ingredients are usually a cheap way to bump up a powder's protein content. In this cookbook, I primarily use whey and pea protein. I also use hemp, though not as frequently due to its more, shall we call it, intense and grassy flavor. I don't use rice protein in this book; neither do I use casein, beef, or egg white proteins. The reason for this is from a nutrition point of view—pea and whey protein cover all the bases. I don't want you to read this book and feel the need to empty out half of your kitchen in order to fit dozens of different tubs of powder. Of course, if you want to experiment beyond whey, pea, and hemp by all means do! There are plenty of different options for and combinations of protein nowadays; feel free to explore them!

SWEETENERS

I use natural sweeteners (like honey, date syrup, or coconut sugar) or low-carb and sugar-free alternatives (like granulated stevia or stevia drops). I prefer these to granulated sucralose or other non-nutritive sweeteners, but feel free to substitute any sweetener you prefer. Just remember, stevia drops are highly concentrated, so when substituting them for other sweeteners, you will need far less.

MEASUREMENTS

The measurements in this book are in cups, tablespoons, and teaspoons. If you'd like to convert them to grams, use this handy guide:

Approximate Conversions

PROTEIN POWDERS

½ cup egg white powder = 48 grams

½ cup pea protein powder = 54 grams

½ cup whey protein powder = 48 grams

½ cup rice protein powder = 62 grams

½ cup hemp protein powder = 62 grams

½ cup casein protein powder = 52 grams

SYRUPS & SWEETENERS

2 tablespoons agave syrup = 38 grams

2 tablespoons honey = 42 grams

2 tablespoons maple syrup = 40 grams

2 tablespoons date syrup = 40 grams

1 tablespoon granulated sweetener = 14 grams

CUPBOARD INGREDIENTS: POWDERED, FLAKED, MILLED

¼ cup coconut sugar = 32 grams

¼ cup cocoa powder = 28 grams

¼ cup coconut flakes = 20 grams

¼ cup grated coconut = 25 grams

¼ cup gluten-free rolled oats = 22 grams

¼ cup ground oats = 32 grams

¼ cup coconut flour = 28 grams

¼ cup defatted almond flour = 35 grams

¼ cup buckwheat flour = 44 grams

¼ cup ground flaxseed = 37 grams

¼ cup buttermilk powder = 40 grams

CUPBOARD INGREDIENTS: NUTS & SEEDS

¼ cup slivered almonds = 20 grams

¼ cup ground almonds = 25–30 grams

¼ cup chopped walnuts = 30 grams

¼ cup chopped pecans = 30 grams

¼ cup chopped cashew nuts = 40 grams

¼ cup pumpkin seeds = 32 grams

¼ cup chia seeds = 40 grams

¼ cup poppy seeds = 36 grams

1 tablespoon nut butter = 16 grams

CUPBOARD INGREDIENTS: CANNED

¼ cup canned pumpkin puree = 55 grams

¼ cup canned chickpeas = 60 grams

¼ cup canned black beans = 63 grams

¼ cup canned pinto beans = 63 grams

CUPBOARD INGREDIENTS: OTHER

¼ cup chocolate chips = 40 grams

¼ cup cocoa nibs = 30 grams

1 square chocolate = 10 grams

¼ cup dried apples = 30 grams

¼ cup goji berries = 33 grams

FRIDGE INGREDIENTS

½ cup milk = 120 ml

1 tablespoon milk = 15 ml

½ cup Greek yogurt = 114 grams

½ cup cottage cheese = 113 grams

¼ cup ricotta cheese = 62 grams

1 fresh egg white = 33 grams

¼ cup liquid egg whites = 2 fresh egg whites = 66 ml

1 large whole egg = 55 grams

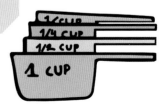

SERVINGS

Since all the recipes in this book are broken down into relatively small (1- to 4-person) servings, you may choose to double or even triple the amount of ingredients for bulk production or to serve several more people.

NUT BUTTERS

As you will see in these recipes, I like to use a lot of nut butters. I use peanut, almond, cashew, and sunflower seed butters often. Bear in mind that different brands of nut butters use different ingredients and have different densities too. As a rule of thumb, I used 100 percent nut butters in all the recipes found in this book. That means I didn't use any nut butters with added sugars or oils. It doesn't mean you have to use 100 percent nut butters, but it does mean that if you use anything other than 100 percent nut butters, you may have to adapt your batter when it comes to the final texture of your bars/truffles/cups. I include pointers in all my directions to make this conversion easier for you.

EQUIPMENT

To make the recipes in this cookbook, I used either a handheld immersion blender, a small food processor, or simply a bowl and a spatula. That's all you need in order to create your own protein-packed snacks. You can use a handheld blender or a regular standing mixer as well. Just don't use a regular blender (you know, a blender designed for shakes or smoothies) to make protein bars, truffles, or mug-cake batters because those blades are very thin and they blend mixtures from the very bottom of the pitcher—so they're not suitable for creating protein doughs—this is especially the case in small batches. However, while they're not fit for doughs, regular blenders work just fine for making protein pancake batters.

GLOVES

When it comes to handling raw protein doughs, and after making probably tens of thousands of protein bars over the years, I learned that a box of (food-safe) gloves can come a long way. These days, I have a box in my kitchen and use them for making all my protein bars and truffles. I suggest you get a box as well. They're cheap and enable you to make your own snacks a lot faster, with less mess and more efficiency.

STORAGE AND DURATION

Once people start making their own protein bars, truffles, and chocolate cups, a frequent question I receive is how they should store them. Here's my answer:

If you want to make a big batch of protein snacks to enjoy for, say, a week or two, make them all in one day and freeze them, wrapping each snack individually. Then, on the day you want to eat your protein bars or truffles, simply defrost them and take them with you! That way they'll be as fresh as possible, every time. You can do this with protein pancakes too! Just make a big batch, freeze them all, and defrost on the day you plan to eat them.

If you don't want to freeze your snacks, simply treat them as you would regular fresh foods: eat them as close to the date you first made them as possible. They're quick and easy enough to prepare that you can make your snacks every day by just making them on the day (or night!) you plan to eat them. If not, store them in an air-tight container in the fridge and enjoy them within three days for maximum freshness.

If you're planning to take your snacks on a day trip or hike, remember that chocolate will melt if you carry it on a hot day. So either coat your snacks with something other than chocolate, or better yet, wrap them in foil and store them in a cooler to ensure you don't end up with a mush! Albeit a delicious one.

PROTEIN BARS

Double Chocolate Bars

Honey and Whey
Protein Bars

Coconut and Whey
Protein Bars

Protein Coffee Bars

Pecan Dark Chocolate
Bars

Vegan Hemp Matcha
Protein Bars

Vegan Chocolate
Protein Bars

Vegan Chocolate Chip
Cookie Dough Bars

Apple Pie Bars

Vegan Almond Cranberry
Protein Bars

Peanut Dark Chocolate
Bars

Hemp Protein Bars

Chocolate Orange Bars

Vegan Cashew Bars

Nut Seed Honey Goji Bars

When it comes to snacking on the go, protein bars are extremely convenient. They're filling, delicious, and (usually) very nutritious, too. Here's the thing though: A lot of bars you find in supermarkets and health-food stores today might as well be called candy, chock-full as they are with simple sugars, preservatives, and nutrition-void ingredients such as corn oil, soy, and hydrogenated fats. In some cases, the only thing you get besides protein is shelf-life-extending ingredients, fillers, and artificial flavors and sweeteners. Your body doesn't really need that stuff. Artificial flavors, artificial sweeteners, E numbers, and an endless array of ingredients that you have probably never otherwise come across are not really anything our bodies are crying out for. Nutrients, sure! But artificial colors and other randomness? Not so much. Sure, many protein bars will say they are "healthy" and "all-natural" on their packaging. You may think they're the best snack your money can buy. But when you turn the label over, you'll find those words are subjective and entirely open to interpretation. The problem, in my opinion, is that most people don't ever read ingredient labels. They stop at macronutrient data (i.e., the nutritional facts). But micros matter too and shouldn't be overlooked. The same can be said about a product's ingredients. They matter.

If you're into healthy snacking and want to incorporate protein into your diet for health and satiety, you really should make your own bars. They're quick to make, fresh every time, and absolutely delicious! In terms of freshness, quality, and nutrition, bars you find on store shelves pale in comparison to what you can make in your kitchen. And the best part? They're silly easy to make and it'll take just as long to prepare them as it would walking to the store and buying a bunch of ready-made bars. You'll end up saving money too.

Here's what a lot of Pow fans do and I suggest you try, at least once, to see whether this is as convenient for you as it is for the thousands of people who do this on a weekly basis: Over a weekend, make a giant batch of protein bars for the next 3–4 days of your work week. When you're done, wrap them all individually in foil, and voila! You get fresh protein bars to enjoy! You can freeze them soon after making so that they last even longer. Take them with you to work, take them with you traveling, to school, on a day out. Take them anywhere you would a regular protein bar and enjoy your very own custom-made bars.

VEGAN HEMP MATCHA PROTEIN BARS

In the past few years, matcha—a high-quality, antioxidant-rich form of powdered green tea—has gotten a lot of attention. Matcha lattes now feature on many popular café menus and if you walk down the aisle of any health-food store, it's hard to avoid powdered matcha. Wherever you see green tea bags, chances are you'll be able to find powdered matcha too. The increased fascination with matcha could be seen as a passing fad, but I think matcha is here to stay. It's a wonderful coffee substitute, and you know what else? It's a phenomenal ingredient in raw snacks as well! Take, for example, these delicious bars.

MAKES 10 BARS

1. In a medium-size bowl, mix all the ingredients except for the dark chocolate using a spatula until you get a dough that you can shape with your hands. If your dough is too wet or sticky, add a bit more of the hemp and/or oats.

2. Divide this dough into 10 balls and then shape them into rectangles. You can do this individually or, if you prefer, you can flatten the entire batch of dough onto a nonstick tray, add a sheet of parchment paper on top, flatten the dough using a rolling pin, and then slice the dough into 10 bars.

3. Melt the dark chocolate in a bain-marie (i.e., a glass bowl on top of a pot of boiling water). Using a spatula (or your hands), dip the bars into the chocolate.

4. Place the chocolate-coated bars onto a nonstick silicone tray or a tray covered with baking paper or aluminum foil. Sprinkle with matcha powder, if desired. Refrigerate for a couple of hours until the chocolate sets or, if you're in a hurry, put them in the freezer for 20 to 30 minutes.

Nutritional data per bar: 169 kcals, 6 grams protein, 17 grams carbs, and 9 grams fat

Bars

½ cup gluten-free rolled oats

6 tablespoons nut butter (I use cashew butter)

½ cup hemp protein

1 tablespoon matcha green tea powder, plus more for topping (optional)

2½ tablespoons agave, honey, or date syrup

4 tablespoons rice milk

⅓ cup pitted medjool dates

Coating

5 squares (50 grams) dark chocolate (90%)

VEGAN CHOCOLATE PROTEIN BARS

After I made these bars, I swear to you, I couldn't stop eating them! So I suggest that you have someone nearby to share them with, or else you might also end up eating them all, too. They are so unbelievably good: like hazelnut-y chocolate cookie dough. You can play around with this recipe by, for example, using cashew instead of almond butter, or adding chocolate chips to the dough. You can also coat the bars in melted dark chocolate if you want to kick things up a notch!

MAKES 8 BARS

1. In a medium-size bowl, mix all the ingredients using a spatula until you get a dough that you can shape with your hands. If your dough is too wet or sticky, add a bit more of the cocoa powder and/or pea protein.

2. Divide this dough into 8 balls and then shape them into rectangles. You can do this individually or, if you prefer, you can flatten the entire batch of dough onto a nonstick tray, put a sheet of parchment paper on top, roll it with a rolling pin, and then slice the dough into 8 bars. That's it, you're done!

Nutritional data per bar: 144 kcals, 10 grams protein, 5 grams carbs, and 9 grams fat

½ cup pea protein powder

5 heaping tablespoons smooth almond butter

4 tablespoons cocoa

2 tablespoons date syrup

6 tablespoons almond milk

¼ cup chopped hazelnuts

Stevia drops to taste (add a couple to your dough to start off with and if, by the end, your mix isn't sweet enough, add a couple more drops of stevia)

VEGAN CHOCOLATE CHIP COOKIE DOUGH BARS

¼ cup smooth peanut butter (or cashew butter)

¼ cup pea protein powder

1 tablespoon granulated stevia

2 tablespoons dark chocolate chips (70-90%)

2 tablespoons almond milk (or cashew milk)

1 tablespoon agave, date, or maple syrup

1 tablespoon coconut flour

The other day I was making protein cookies, ate a bunch of the dough, and then looked down at what I was about to put into my preheated oven: a tray with two sad cookies on it. Why sad? Because they were lonely. Why lonely? Because I'd eaten most of the dough. I ended up just turning off the oven and eating the remaining cookie dough raw. It had to be done, you know? Because who bakes just TWO cookies?

MAKES 6 BARS

1. In a medium-size bowl, mix all the ingredients together with a spatula until you get a dough that you can shape with your hands. If your dough is too wet or sticky, add a bit more of the pea protein powder and/or almond flour. Taste it to ensure it's sweet enough for you.

2. Divide this dough into 6 balls and then shape them into rectangles. You can do this individually or, if you prefer, you can flatten the entire batch of dough onto a nonstick tray, put a sheet of parchment paper on top, roll it with a rolling pin, and then slice the dough into 6 bars.

3. Place the bars onto a nonstick silicone tray or a tray covered with baking paper or aluminum foil. Refrigerate for a couple of hours or, if you're in a hurry, put them in the freezer for 20 to 30 minutes.

Nutritional data per bar: 169 kcals, 11 grams protein, 7 grams carbs, and 10 grams fat

CONSIDER ADDING CRANBERRIES OR SOME CHOPPED NUTS.

APPLE PIE BARS

I've long been a fan of cinnamon and apples. When I was growing up, one of my favorite things my mom would make was steamed apples with just a tiny bit of cinnamon and sliced almonds on top. Such a simple snack! I used to mix the apples into my yogurt or just enjoy them in a bowl—sweet and delicious. That love for cinnamon, apples, and almonds inspired these bars. If you want to add an extra element of crunch, feel free to add chopped walnuts or pecans to your dough. And if you want to take things to the next level (if, say, you're making these for a loved one or feel like making them into more of a treat for yourself), you could coat them with melted white chocolate too. Just an idea for those of you who like to push the boundaries of **POW**.

¼ cup pea protein powder

¼ cup almond butter

¼ cup almond flour

5 tablespoons almond milk

2 tablespoons chopped dried apple

1 tablespoon agave, date, or maple syrup

1 tablespoon vanilla extract

Cinnamon, to taste

MAKES 8 BARS

1. In a food processor, combine all the ingredients until you get a firm dough that you can shape with your hands. If your dough is too wet or sticky, add a bit more of the pea protein powder and/or almond flour.

2. Divide this dough into 8 balls and then shape them into rectangles. You can do this individually or, if you prefer, you can flatten the entire batch of dough onto a nonstick tray, put a sheet of parchment paper on top, roll it with a rolling pin, and then slice the dough into 8 bars.

Nutritional data per bar: 100 kcals, 7 grams protein, 7 grams carbs, and 5 grams fat

DOUBLE CHOCOLATE BARS

Bars

¼ cup whey protein powder

2 tablespoons coconut flour

2 tablespoons coconut sugar (or your low-carb sweetener of choice)

2 tablespoons almond milk

1½ tablespoons smooth peanut butter

2 tablespoons cocoa powder

Coating

4 squares (40 grams) dark chocolate (90%)

1-2 tablespoons chopped nuts (optional, but nice for an extra crunch)

Over the last five years, I've published thousands of protein recipes online. Among them, do you know how many feature chocolate? Over 60 percent. Yeah, I was pretty shocked when I found out. Shocked but not surprised, because I am a self-proclaimed chocoholic. I just adore chocolate, especially dark chocolate! And if you do too, well, then these bars are for you. They're really easy and, like all my other recipes, open to a lot of variations. You can, for example, use almond butter instead of peanut butter. You can leave your bars naked—i.e., not coat them in dark chocolate. You can even roll the dough into balls and roll them in cocoa powder to make delicious truffles. Try different ways of approaching this dough, customize it to your taste buds, and enjoy!

MAKES 4 BARS

1. In a food processor or in a medium-size bowl using a spatula, combine all the ingredients, except for the dark chocolate and chopped nuts, until you get a firm dough you can shape with your hands. If your dough is too wet or sticky, add a bit more of the whey protein powder and/or coconut flour.

2. Divide this dough into 4 balls and then shape them into rectangles. You can do this individually or, if you prefer, you can flatten the entire batch of dough onto a nonstick tray, put a sheet of parchment paper on top, roll it with a rolling pin, and then slice the dough into 4 bars.

3. Melt the dark chocolate in a bain-marie (i.e., a glass bowl on top of a pot of boiling water).

4. Using a spatula (or your hands), dip the bars into the chocolate.

5. Place the chocolate-coated bars onto a nonstick silicone tray or a tray covered with baking paper or aluminum foil. Sprinkle with chopped nuts, if using. Refrigerate for a couple of hours until the chocolate sets or, if you're in a hurry, put them in the freezer for 20 to 30 minutes.

Nutritional data per bar: 162 kcals, 10 grams protein, 11 grams carbs, and 10 grams fat

HONEY AND WHEY PROTEIN BARS

You know when you make a recipe and it looks too pretty to eat? You really want to dig in but you also want to keep taking photos? Yeah, I couldn't stop shooting these bars after I made them. I was torn between a strong desire to devour them and a powerful urge to photograph them from different angles. They're extremely easy-to-make protein bars. All you need are a few very basic ingredients and **POW!** You end up with little delicious bars that you can look at—and then demolish with gusto!

MAKES 4 BARS

1. In a food processor or in a medium-size bowl using a spatula, combine all the ingredients, except for the dark chocolate, until you get a firm dough you can shape with your hands.

2. Divide this dough into 4 balls and then shape them into rectangles. You can do this individually or, if you prefer, you can flatten the entire batch of dough onto a nonstick tray, put a sheet of parchment paper on top, roll it with a rolling pin, and then slice the dough into 4 bars.

3. Melt the dark chocolate in a bain-marie (i.e., a glass bowl on top of a pot of boiling water).

4. Using a spatula (or your hands), dip the bars into the chocolate.

5. Place the chocolate-coated bars onto a nonstick silicone tray or a tray covered with baking paper or aluminum foil. Refrigerate for a couple of hours until the chocolate sets or, if you're in a hurry, put them in the freezer for 20 to 30 minutes.

Nutritional data per bar: 141 kcals, 9 grams protein, 8 grams carbs, and 9 grams fat

Bars

2 tablespoons almond butter

¼ cup whey protein

1 tablespoon honey

1 tablespoon milk (almond, rice, cow—any milk)

1 tablespoon coconut flour

Coating

3 squares (30 grams) dark chocolate (90%)

COCONUT AND WHEY PROTEIN BARS

Bars

¼ cup whey protein

¼ cup plus 1 tablespoon coconut flakes, plus more for topping

2 tablespoons coconut flour

½–1 teaspoon stevia drops (or your low-carb sweetener of choice)

2 tablespoons almond milk

Coating

3 squares (30 grams) dark chocolate (90%)

I've made these bars more times than I can count after creating the recipe for this book. They're just so quick and easy! And if you love coconut as much as I do, you're in for a treat, literally. They're crunchy, coconutty, and the perfect protein tribute to Bounty or Mound candy bars!

MAKES 3 BARS

1. In a medium bowl using a spatula, combine all the ingredients, except for the dark chocolate, until you get a dough you can shape with your hands. If your dough is too wet or sticky, add a bit more of the coconut flour.

2. Divide this dough into 3 small balls and then shape them into rectangles. You can do this individually or, if you prefer, you can flatten the entire batch of dough onto a nonstick tray, put a sheet of parchment paper on top, roll it with a rolling pin, and then slice the dough into 3 bars.

3. Melt the dark chocolate in a bain-marie (i.e., a glass bowl on top of a pot of boiling water).

4. Using a spatula (or your hands), dip the bars into the chocolate. Note, if your bars are too soft, simply pour the melted chocolate on top.

5. Place the chocolate-coated bars onto a nonstick silicone tray or a tray covered with baking paper or aluminum foil. Add a few extra coconut flakes on top. Refrigerate for a couple of hours until the chocolate sets or, if you're in a hurry, put them in the freezer for 20 to 30 minutes.

Nutritional data per bar: 151 kcals, 11 grams protein, 6 grams carbs, and 11 grams fat

PROTEIN COFFEE BARS

Did you know that medjool dates are nature's candy? They are! If you mush them up to create a paste, they're a fantastic substitute for caramel. I use them a lot and I invite you to do the same. The dates add texture, sweetness, and make your protein bars taste like candy!

MAKES 4 BARS

1. In a medium bowl using a spatula and then your hands, combine all the ingredients, except for the dates and dark chocolate, until you get a soft dough. If your dough is too wet or sticky, add a bit more of the ground almonds.

2. Divide this dough into 4 balls and then shape them into rectangles. You can do this individually or, if you prefer, you can flatten the entire batch of dough onto a nonstick tray, put a sheet of parchment paper on top, roll it with a rolling pin, and then slice the dough into 4 bars.

3. Place the bars onto a nonstick silicone tray or a tray covered with baking paper or aluminum foil. Set in the fridge for 30 minutes.

4. Place your medjool dates in a small food processor until you get a soft caramel-like paste. Spread this date paste onto your 4 bars.

5. Melt the dark chocolate in a bain-marie (i.e., a glass bowl on top of a pot of boiling water). Pour the melted chocolate over your bars. Refrigerate for a couple of hours until the chocolate sets or, if you're in a hurry, put them in the freezer for 20 to 30 minutes.

Nutritional data per bar: 209 kcals, 8 grams protein, 13 grams carbs, and 14 grams fat

Bars

1 teaspoon freshly brewed coffee (espresso)

2 tablespoons almond butter

½ cup ground almonds

1 tablespoon agave, date, or maple syrup

¼ cup whey protein

Coating

2 pitted medjool dates

4 squares (40 grams) dark chocolate (70–90%)

PECAN DARK CHOCOLATE BARS

Bars

¼ cup whey protein powder

1 tablespoon coconut sugar (see note)

¼ cup pecan halves, plus more for optional topping

1 tablespoon almond milk

1 teaspoon maple extract

¼ cup ground almonds

½ tablespoon agave or maple syrup

Coating

2 squares (20 grams) dark chocolate (70-90%)

Note: *Replace the coconut sugar with granulated stevia, if you want your bars to be lower in carbs.*

Let's say you're at work and you're feeling a bit bored. You're looking at the clock and the minutes seem to last forever. You're tired, sleepy, and impatiently waiting for something to zap you into life. Your stomach growls, you're hungry. But you don't want a huge or massively caloric meal because you know that'll make you even sleepier. You need some kind of pick-me-up. **POW!** Enter these bars! They're sweet, chocolatey, and delicious. Enjoy them alongside a big cup of coffee in the afternoon. These bars will lift you up and superpower you through the day!

MAKES 3 BARS

1. In a food processor, mix all the ingredients together, except for the dark chocolate, until you get a dough that you can shape with your hands. If your dough is too wet or sticky, add a bit more ground almonds.

2. Divide this dough into 3 balls and then shape them into rectangles. You can do this individually or, if you prefer, you can flatten the entire batch of dough onto a nonstick tray, put a sheet of parchment paper on top, roll it with a rolling pin, and then slice the dough into 3 bars.

3. Melt the dark chocolate in a bain-marie (i.e., a glass bowl on top of a pot of boiling water).

4. Using a spatula (or your hands), dip the bars into the chocolate.

5. Place the bars onto a nonstick silicone tray or a tray covered with baking paper or aluminum foil. Add some extra pecans on top and drizzle with extra chocolate (if you want). Refrigerate for a couple of hours until the chocolate sets or, if you're in a hurry, put them in the freezer for 20 to 30 minutes.

Nutritional data per bar: 191 kcals, 9.5 grams protein, 7 grams carbs, and 13.8 grams fat

VEGAN ALMOND CRANBERRY PROTEIN BARS

These bars are extremely quick and easy to make. Well, I guess all my protein bars are, but these ones are especially simple. Just get a bowl out, chuck all your ingredients in, and make a delicious dough to shape into bars. If you want to tweak the recipe as you go along, go for it! Consider, for example, melting some dark chocolate on top and adding more walnuts to your dough. Or adding some sugar-free white chocolate chips.

MAKES 6 BARS

1. In a food processor, combine all your ingredients, except for the cranberries and dark chocolate, until you get a firm dough you can shape with your hands. If your dough is too wet or sticky, add a bit more of the ground almonds.

2. Add the cranberries and chopped chocolate to your dough.

3. Divide this dough into 6 balls and then shape them into rectangles. You can do this individually or, if you prefer, you can flatten the entire batch of dough onto a nonstick tray, put a sheet of parchment paper on top, roll it with a rolling pin, and then slice the dough into 6 bars.

4. Place the bars onto a nonstick silicone tray or a tray covered with baking paper or aluminum foil. Refrigerate for a couple of hours or, if you're in a hurry, put them in the freezer for 20 to 30 minutes.

Nutritional data per bar: 139 kcals, 8 grams protein, 7 grams carbs, and 9 grams fat

¼ cup pea protein powder

3 tablespoons almond butter

2 tablespoons agave, date, or maple syrup

3 tablespoons almond milk

3 tablespoons ground almonds

1 tablespoon cranberries

1 square (10 grams) dark chocolate (70-90%), chopped

PEANUT DARK CHOCOLATE BARS

Bars

¼ cup whey protein powder

2 tablespoons granulated stevia (or coconut sugar)

1 tablespoon cocoa powder

3 tablespoons defatted peanut flour

4 tablespoons almond milk (or your milk of choice)

2 tablespoons coconut flour

Coating

4 squares (40 grams) dark chocolate (70-90%)

Chopped nuts, for topping (optional)

Defatted peanut flour is a flour derived from crushed peanuts in which a quantity of the fat has been removed. It's a pretty unusual ingredient. Some people add a bit of water to it, turn it into a paste, and use it as a peanut butter substitute—but that doesn't do it for me at all. It's more paste than butter that way, you know? That doesn't mean I dislike peanut flour; in fact, I love it! But only as flour, not as a peanut butter substitute. Peanut flour, used in raw protein snacks and/or baking, lends a really nice and mildly nutty flavor to food. I urge you to try it, experiment with it, and see what you think. If you don't have or want it, though, feel free to make this recipe by substituting the peanut flour with almond flour. Obviously your bars won't be Peanut Dark Chocolate Bars, but they'll be just as good!

MAKES 3 BARS

1. In a medium-size bowl with a spatula, mix all the ingredients together, except for the dark chocolate, until you get a dough you can shape with your hands. If your dough is too wet or sticky, add a bit more of the cocoa, coconut flour, or peanut flour.

2. Divide this dough into 3 balls and then shape them into rectangles. You can do this individually or, if you prefer, you can flatten the entire batch of dough onto a nonstick tray, put a sheet of parchment paper on top, roll it with a rolling pin, and then slice the dough into 3 bars.

3. Melt the dark chocolate in a bain-marie (i.e., a glass bowl on top of a pot of boiling water).

continued

4. Using a spatula (or your hands), dip the bars into the chocolate.

5. Place the bars onto a nonstick silicone tray or a tray covered with baking paper or aluminum foil. You can garnish the bars with chopped nuts like I did, or leave them plain. Refrigerate for a couple of hours until the chocolate sets or, if you're in a hurry, put them in the freezer for 20 to 30 minutes.

Nutritional data per bar: 173 kcals, 14 grams protein, 7 grams carbs, and 9 grams fat

DON'T LIKE PEANUTS? MAKE THIS RECIPE WITH DEFATTED ALMOND FLOUR INSTEAD!

HEMP PROTEIN BARS

People often ask me about hemp protein powder: Can it be used as a substitute for whey protein in recipes? Can it be used as a substitute for pea protein or rice? My answer is always the same: It depends. You see, from a nutritional point of view, hemp protein powder is amazing and its texture is very much like other veggie protein powders, so when it comes to baking, it won't dry your foods or make them rubbery and hard. But because of its . . . shall we call it unique flavor, hemp protein requires special treatment. It's less versatile than whey or pea protein powder because it tastes very strongly of grass. So it's hard to truly mask its flavor. That's why the only time I recommend people use hemp is when it comes to very chocolatey bars or truffles. There, the hemp flavor can actually complement dark chocolate very nicely! But don't take my word for it—make these bars and see what you think!

MAKES 4 BARS

1. In a medium-size bowl, mix all the ingredients together, except for the dark chocolate, until you get a dough that you can shape with your hands. Feel free to add even more hulled hemp seeds if you like their nuttiness! Or throw in some dried fruit or nuts—anything goes. If your dough is too wet or sticky, add a bit more of the cocoa powder or coconut flour.

2. Divide this dough into 4 balls and then shape them into rectangles. You can do this individually or, if you prefer, you can flatten the entire batch of dough onto a nonstick tray, put a sheet of parchment paper on top, roll it with a rolling pin, and then slice the dough into 4 bars.

3. Melt the dark chocolate in a bain-marie (i.e., a glass bowl on top of a pot of boiling water).

continued

Bars

¼ cup hemp protein

2 tablespoons cocoa powder

2–3 tablespoons agave, maple, or date syrup

4 tablespoons almond butter

2 tablespoons almond milk

2 tablespoons coconut flour

2 tablespoons hulled hemp seeds, plus more for an optional topping

Coating

5 squares (50 grams) dark chocolate (70–85%)

4. Using a spatula (or your hands), cover the bottom and sides of each bar with chocolate.

5. Place the chocolate-coated bars onto a nonstick silicone tray or a tray covered with baking paper or aluminum foil. Add some extra hulled hemp seeds on top. This is optional but it's a great way to add extra hemp to your bars!

6. Refrigerate for a couple of hours until the chocolate sets or, if you're in a hurry, put them in the freezer for 20 to 30 minutes.

Nutritional data per bar: 261 kcals, 13 grams protein, 12 grams carbs, and 19 grams fat

CHOCOLATE ORANGE BARS

Bars

¼ cup whey protein

1 teaspoon stevia drops (or your low-carb sweetener of choice)

1 tablespoon cashew or almond butter

2 tablespoons coconut flour

1 tablespoon ground almonds

½ tablespoon cocoa powder

2 tablespoons almond milk

½ tablespoon orange zest

Coating

5 squares (50 grams) dark chocolate (85%)

I add orange zest to a lot of my (sweet) food: my morning oatmeal, smoothies, rice puddings, protein truffles, and bars. It's a wonderful ingredient! Whenever I host a Protein Pow workshop, I bring a bunch of oranges and zesters and love to watch people discover how orange zest transforms their snacks by adding a delicious fragrance and tangy flavor to them. Orange zest is great to add to both vanilla and chocolate bars. If you've never tried it, a good place to start is right here.

MAKES 5 BARS

1. In a large bowl with a spatula, mix your whey protein, stevia, nut butter, coconut flour, ground almonds, cocoa powder, almond milk, and ¼ tablespoon of the orange zest until you get a dough you can shape with your hands. If your dough is too wet or sticky, add a bit more of the cocoa powder. If it's too dry, add a bit of milk.

2. Divide this dough into 5 small balls and then shape them into rectangles. You can do this individually or, if you prefer, you can flatten the entire batch of dough onto a nonstick tray, put a sheet of parchment paper on top, roll it with a rolling pin, and then slice the dough into 5 bars.

3. Transfer the bars to the fridge for 20 minutes or the freezer for 10 minutes. This allows them to harden up a bit and they become easier to coat.

4. Melt the dark chocolate in a bain-marie (i.e., a glass bowl on top of a pot of boiling water).

5. Using a spatula (or your hands), dip the bars into the chocolate.

6. Place the chocolate-coated bars onto a nonstick silicone tray or a tray covered with baking paper or aluminum foil. Top the bars with the remaining orange zest. Stick them in the freezer for an hour and . . . **POW!** They're ready!

Nutritional data per bar: 118 kcals, 8 grams protein, 4 grams carbs, and 8 grams fat

VEGAN CASHEW BARS

These bars are really soft and doughy, like cashew nut cookie dough! They're a great base for other ingredients. For example, you can add chocolate chips, protein puffs, nuts, or dried fruit to your dough. If you happen to not like (or have) cashew butter and/or cashews, feel free to use almonds instead. Your texture will be different, of course, but the result will be just as delicious!

MAKES 5 BARS

1. In a big bowl, mix all the ingredients together, except for the dark chocolate, until you have a soft dough. If your dough is too soft or sticky, add a bit more of the ground almonds until you get a mixture that you can shape with your hands.

2. Divide this dough into 5 small balls and then shape them into rectangles. You can do this individually or, if you prefer, you can flatten the entire batch of dough onto a nonstick tray, put a sheet of parchment paper on top, roll it with a rolling pin, and then slice the dough into 5 bars.

3. Melt the dark chocolate in a bain-marie (i.e., a glass bowl on top of a pot of boiling water).

4. Using a spatula (or your hands), cover the bottom and sides of each bar with chocolate.

5. Add your cashew halves, if using, on top of each bar. Pour the rest of the chocolate on top.

6. Place the chocolate-coated bars onto a nonstick silicone tray or a tray covered with baking paper or aluminum foil. Refrigerate for a couple of hours until the chocolate sets or, if you're in a hurry, put them in the freezer for 20 to 30 minutes.

Nutritional data per bar: 135 kcals, 6 grams protein, 6 grams carbs, and 10 grams fat

Bars

2 tablespoons cashew butter

1 tablespoon agave or maple syrup, or your low-carb sweetener of choice

2 tablespoons pea protein powder

1/4 cup ground almonds

1 tablespoon cashew milk

Coating

4 squares (40 grams) dark chocolate (70–85%)

5 cashew halves (optional but nice for extra crunch)

NUT SEED HONEY GOJI BARS

Bars

¼ cup goji berries, plus more for topping

¼ cup pumpkin seeds

¼ cup chopped nuts, plus more for topping

1 tablespoon honey

2 tablespoons pea protein powder

2 tablespoons cashew butter

1 tablespoon milk

Coating

5 squares (50 grams) dark chocolate (85%)

10 squares (100 grams) white chocolate (optional)

These bars are very unusual. You have to use a food processor to make them, so they take a tiny bit longer than other bar recipes in the book. But don't let that extra equipment keep you from making them, because these bars are GOOD. They're unbelievably crunchy and sweet, and are the perfect bars to take with you if you're going on a long hike or day out because they're harder than my cookie-doughy filled bars.

MAKES 6 BARS

1. In a small food processor, combine all the ingredients, except for the chocolate, until you get a dough that you can shape with your hands. If the dough is too wet or sticky, add a bit more pea protein powder.

2. Divide this dough into 6 small balls and then shape them into rectangles. You can do this individually or, if you prefer, you can flatten the entire batch of dough onto a nonstick tray, put a sheet of parchment paper on top, roll it with a rolling pin, and then slice the dough into 6 bars.

3. Melt the dark chocolate in a bain-marie (i.e., a glass bowl on top of a pot of boiling water).

4. Using a spatula (or your hands), dip the bars into the chocolate.

5. Top with some extra goji berries, chopped nuts, and some melted white chocolate (if you'd like).

6. Place the chocolate-coated bars onto a nonstick silicone tray or a tray covered with baking paper or aluminum foil. Refrigerate for a couple of hours until the chocolate sets or, if you're in a hurry, put them in the freezer for 20 to 30 minutes.

Nutritional data per bar: 178 kcals, 8 grams protein, 10 grams carbs, and 12 grams fat

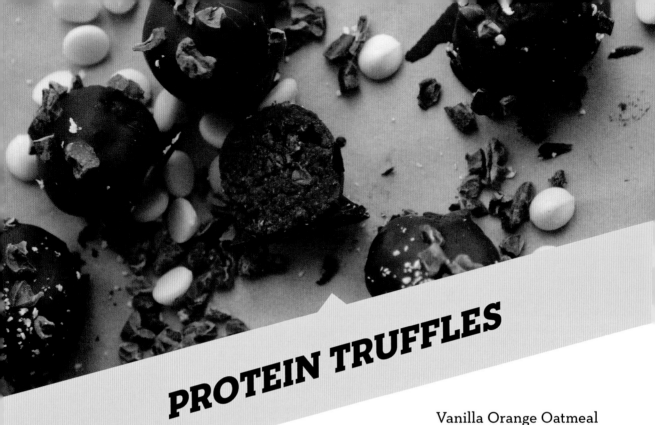

PROTEIN TRUFFLES

Chocolate Chip Cookie
Dough Truffles

Strawberry Shortcake
Whey Truffles

Peanut Butter and Jelly
Truffles

Peanut Butter and
Chocolate Protein Truffles

Dark Chocolate Almond
Truffles

Dark Chocolate Goji
Truffles

White Chocolate and
Lemon Zest Protein
Truffles

Vegan Double-Chocolate
Protein Truffles

Matcha and Coconut
Protein Truffles

Vegan Cocoa Pow Truffles

Macadamia Energy
Truffles

Chocolate Coconut
Energy Truffles

Spice and All Things Nice
Truffles

Vanilla Orange Oatmeal
Truffles

Cocoa Nibs Coffee
Truffles

Almond Cranberry
Protein Truffles

Dark Chocolate and
Almond Mania Protein
Truffles

Hemp Cocoa Dark
Chocolate Truffles

Sunflower Honey Protein
Truffles

Coffee Protein Truffles

Protein truffles are a great alternative to protein bars in that they're another fantastic snack to make and enjoy during your day as a treat, a healthy nibble to graze on between meals, or a little bite of dessert to have after dinner.

When it comes to making them, protein truffles are actually a bit easier than protein bars because all you need to do is roll up your dough—you don't have to shape it into bars. If you decide to coat them in melted chocolate, protein truffles are easier to dunk into your chocolate and coat since they have less surface area than bars and are thus less likely to fall apart inside the melted chocolate.

There are many ways of coating your truffles and bars beyond melted dark chocolate and cocoa powder in case you don't like or (for some reason) are not in the mood for chocolate. You can roll them in chopped nuts, ground nuts, or chopped seeds. I personally love pulsing almonds with brazil nuts and using that as a coating. Ground sunflower seeds are also a great alternative. Another thing you can do is roll the dough in cinnamon and coconut sugar or granulated stevia or an erythritol-based powdered sweetener for more of a sweet "sugar" coating.

Please do experiment as you go along—take my recipes and turn them on their head if you wish. Tweak them. Change them. Adapt them to your unique flavor and taste preferences. Make them yours! It's what it's about at the end of the day: playing with food and having fun in the kitchen as you make your healthy snacks!

CHOCOLATE CHIP COOKIE DOUGH TRUFFLES

This recipe is incredibly quick and easy to follow: All you need to do is grab a handful of ingredients, throw them in a bowl, press them into a dough, and roll that dough into balls. Easy. And you end up with delicious bites of cookie doughy goodness! What's not to love, right?

MAKES 8 TRUFFLES

1. In a medium-size bowl with a spatula, combine all your ingredients until you get a dough that you can shape with your hands. If your dough is too wet or sticky, add a bit more of the coconut flour.

2. Roll the dough into 8 truffles.

Nutritional data per truffle: 95 kcals, 5 grams protein, 4 grams carbs, and 6 grams fat

¼ cup whey protein powder

2 tablespoons coconut flour

¼ cup cashew butter

1 heaping tablespoon agave, date, or maple syrup

2 tablespoons dark chocolate chips

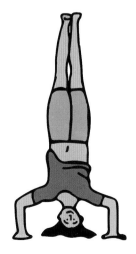

STRAWBERRY SHORTCAKE WHEY TRUFFLES

These protein truffles are a tribute to strawberry shortcake, one of my all-time favorite cakes. I use freeze-dried strawberries to make them. Freeze-dried strawberries, or any freeze-dried fruits really, are a fantastic ingredient to make snacks with because they're 100 percent fruit! Nothing else is added to them. Unlike dried fruits, which often contain extra sugars and are pretty chewy, freeze-dried fruits are extremely light and airy while delivering a punch of fruity deliciousness. Give them a go if you haven't already!

MAKES 16 TRUFFLES

1. In a medium-size bowl with a spatula, add all your ingredients together until you get a soft dough. If your dough is too wet or sticky, add a bit more of the coconut flour.

2. Roll your dough into 16 truffles.

Nutritional data per truffle: 59 kcals, 3 grams protein, 4 grams carbs, and 3 grams fat

½ cup almond butter

¼ cup whey protein powder

1 small handful freeze-dried strawberries (or dried fruit, if you can't find freeze-dried berries)

¼ cup cream cheese

1 tablespoon granulated stevia (or your low-carb sweetener of choice)

½ cup ground gluten-free oats (either purchased ground or ground up in a food processor)

3½ tablespoons coconut flour

1 teaspoon vanilla extract

TO MAKE THESE TRUFFLES EVEN MORE OF A TREAT, CONSIDER COATING THEM IN MELTED DARK (OR WHITE) CHOCOLATE!

PEANUT BUTTER AND JELLY TRUFFLES

3 tablespoons smooth peanut butter

¼ cup whey protein powder

4 tablespoons reduced-sugar strawberry jam

3 tablespoons coconut flour

¼ cup oat flour

1 teaspoon stevia drops

Imagine having a magic wand that turns your food dreams into reality. You see a peanut butter and jelly sandwich and *tliiiing* you turn it into truffles. Then *tliiiing* you turn those truffles into a functional food by adding protein and reducing any/all sugars. The results? Bite-size pieces of peanut butter and jelly that pack a protein punch!

MAKES 9 TRUFFLES

1. In a medium-size bowl with a spatula, add all your ingredients together until you get a soft dough. If your dough is too wet or sticky, add a bit more of the coconut flour.

2. Roll your dough into 9 truffles.

Nutritional data per truffle: 79 kcals, 5 grams protein, 8 grams carbs, and 3 grams fat

PEANUT BUTTER AND CHOCOLATE PROTEIN TRUFFLES

This is one of the first recipes I ever made using whey protein powder. It's quick, easy, and absolutely delicious! I normally make a bunch of these truffles and take them with me to the office, in a little Tupperware I call my "truffleware" to enjoy alongside my coffee in the afternoon when the cravings for something sweet kick in.

MAKES 6 TRUFFLES

1. In a medium-size bowl with a spatula, mix all your ingredients together, except for the dark chocolate, until you get a soft dough that you can shape with your hands. If your mixture is too wet or sticky, add a bit more coconut flour.

2. Roll your dough into 6 truffles.

3. Melt the dark chocolate in a bain-marie (i.e., a glass bowl on top of a pot of boiling water).

4. Using a spatula (or your hands), dip the truffles into the chocolate.

5. Place the chocolate-coated truffles onto a nonstick silicone tray or a tray covered with baking paper or aluminum foil. Refrigerate for a couple of hours until the chocolate sets or, if you're in a hurry, put them in the freezer for 20 to 30 minutes.

Optional: *If you want to add some peanut butter swirls on top, just melt a tablespoon of smooth peanut butter and 1 teaspoon of coconut oil in the microwave for 20 seconds, then stick it in a piping bag with a thin nozzle (or a plastic sandwich bag with the corner cut off), and decorate the truffles to your liking.*

Nutritional data per truffle: 111 kcals, 6 grams protein, 5 grams carbs, and 7 grams fat

Truffles

2 tablespoons smooth peanut butter

¼ cup whey protein powder

2 tablespoons coconut flour

1 tablespoon honey

1 tablespoon almond milk

Coating

2 squares (20 grams) dark chocolate

DARK CHOCOLATE ALMOND TRUFFLES

2 tablespoons whey protein powder

¼ cup plus 2 tablespoons ground almonds

2 tablespoons almond butter

1 tablespoon cocoa powder

1 tablespoon agave, maple, or date syrup

1 tablespoon almond milk

1 tablespoon cocoa powder, plus more for coating

Soft, doughy, chocolatey truffles. Coated in 100 percent cocoa powder. These truffles are a chocolate lover's dream come true! These are the perfect post-dinner snack when you feel like having something sweet but low in calories after your dinner. Just a bit of **POW!** to satisfy your sweet tooth.

MAKES 8 TRUFFLES

1. In a medium-size bowl with a spatula, add all your ingredients together until you get a soft dough. If your dough is too wet or sticky, add a bit more of the ground almonds and/or cocoa powder.

2. Roll the dough into 8 truffles.

3. Pour some cocoa powder into a bowl and coat your truffles with it!

Nutritional data per truffle: 61 kcals, 3 grams protein, 2 grams carbs, and 5 grams fat

DARK CHOCOLATE GOJI TRUFFLES

These little truffles are packed full of nutritious ingredients. They're also delicious and a wonderful little snack to take with you on a hike, a day out, to work, or to school. Just wrap them in foil or carry them inside a little airtight container to enjoy whenever you most need a healthy, sweet snack!

MAKES 10 TRUFFLES

1. In a food processor, pulse all your ingredients together until you get a soft dough. If your dough is too wet or sticky, add a bit more of the ground almonds and/or cocoa powder.

2. Roll your dough into 8 truffles.

3. Pour some cocoa powder into a bowl and coat your truffles with it!

Nutritional data per truffle: 69 kcals, 5 grams protein, 6 grams carbs, and 3 grams fat

3 tablespoons sunflower seeds

3 tablespoons hulled hemp seeds

¼ cup pea protein powder

2 tablespoons coconut sugar

¼ cup goji berries

3 tablespoons hemp, rice, or almond milk

½ tablespoon granulated stevia (or your low-carb sweetener of choice)

2 tablespoons cocoa powder, plus more for coating

IF YOU'D LIKE AN EXTRA ELEMENT OF CRUNCH, ADD SOME SUGAR-FREE WHITE CHOCOLATE CHIPS, CHOPPED PECANS, OR CHOPPED WALNUTS TO YOUR DOUGH.

WHITE CHOCOLATE AND LEMON ZEST PROTEIN TRUFFLES

¼ cup whey protein powder

3½ tablespoons coconut flour

2 tablespoons granulated stevia (or your low-carb sweetener of choice)

2 tablespoons cashew or almond milk

Lemon zest from ¼ lemon

2–3 tablespoons sugar-free white chocolate chips (or sprinkles or coconut flakes)

Lemon zest, like orange zest, lends a nice tangy flavor to protein bars and truffles. Just bear in mind, when you're buying lemons to zest, that you should purchase unwaxed lemons—or if you do buy waxed lemons, you should give them a good scrub before zesting. You don't want to eat wax with your zest. Why are there even waxed lemons out there? Waxing lemons extends their shelf life by a good two to three weeks if stored at room temperature.

MAKES 6 TRUFFLES

1. In a medium-size bowl with a spatula, add all your ingredients together, except the white chocolate chips, until you get a soft dough. If your dough is too wet or sticky, add a bit more of the coconut flour. If your dough is too dry or crumbly, add a bit more milk.

2. Roll your dough into 6 truffles.

3. Pour some sugar-free white chocolate chips (or sprinkles or coconut flakes) into a bowl and roll the truffles through it!

Nutritional data per truffle: 34 kcals, 4 grams protein, 3 grams carbs, and 1 gram fat

VEGAN DOUBLE-CHOCOLATE PROTEIN TRUFFLES

These truffles are irresistible. Be warned—you'll want to eat them all. Make sure you either make small quantities, you have someone around to help you, or you freeze most of them right after making them, because you really will want to eat them all. They are really tasty. Like . . . soft almond chocolate cookie dough! I dare you to make them and not fall head over heels in love.

MAKES 8 TRUFFLES

1. In a medium-size bowl with a spatula, mix all your ingredients together, except for the dark chocolate, until you get a soft dough that you can shape with your hands. If your mixture is too wet or sticky, add a bit more coconut flour.

2. Roll your dough into 8 truffles.

3. Melt the dark chocolate in a bain-marie (i.e., a glass bowl on top of a pot of boiling water).

4. Using a spatula (or your hands), dip the truffles into the chocolate.

5. Place the chocolate-coated truffles onto a nonstick silicone tray or a tray covered with baking paper or aluminum foil. Refrigerate for a couple of hours until the chocolate sets or, if you're in a hurry, put them in the freezer for 20 to 30 minutes.

Nutritional data per truffle: 71 kcals, 3 grams protein, 3 grams carbs, and 7 grams fat

Truffles

2 tablespoons ground almonds

2 teaspoons melted coconut oil

2 tablespoons cocoa powder

3 tablespoons almond milk

½ teaspoon stevia drops

2 tablespoons pea protein powder

1 tablespoon coconut sugar

Coating

5 squares (50 grams) dark chocolate (90%)

TOP WITH COCONUT FLAKES FOR EXTRA POW!

MATCHA AND COCONUT PROTEIN TRUFFLES

Truffles

3 tablespoons coconut flour

2 tablespoons almond milk

¼ cup whey protein powder

1 teaspoon matcha, plus more for topping

1 tablespoon granulated truvia (or your low-carb sweetener of choice)

¼ cup coconut flakes

Coating

5 squares (50 grams) dark chocolate

Green tea and coconut are two flavors that go extremely well together. Have you ever had a matcha latte made with coconut milk? It's delicious! And there are other desserts out there too that combine green tea and coconut to perfection, e.g. matcha coconut pudding and matcha coconut cake. If you've never had them, let these protein truffles introduce you to the world of matcha and coconut. It's a tasty world worth delving into.

MAKES 7 TRUFFLES

1. In a small food processor, mix all your ingredients together, except for the dark chocolate, until you get a soft dough that you can shape with your hands. If your mixture is too wet or sticky, add a bit more coconut flour.

2. Roll your dough into 7 truffles.

3. Melt the dark chocolate in a bain-marie (i.e., a glass bowl on top of a pot of boiling water).

4. Using a spatula (or your hands), dip the truffles into the chocolate.

5. Place the chocolate-coated truffles onto a nonstick silicone tray or a tray covered with baking paper or aluminum foil. Sprinkle some matcha on top. Refrigerate for a couple of hours until the chocolate sets or, if you're in a hurry, put them in the freezer for 20 to 30 minutes.

Nutritional data per truffle: 77 kcals, 4 grams protein, 3 grams carbs, and 5 grams fat

VEGAN COCOA POW TRUFFLES

At this stage of the game, you may be thinking, "Moses, Anna, another cocoa/chocolate recipe?!" It's true—there are a lot of them in this book. But I promise you, they're all very unique! And if you're as into chocolate as I am, they're all absolutely worth making. You can never really have too much chocolate in life anyway, right? Hehe.

MAKES 8 TRUFFLES

1. In a medium-size bowl with a spatula, add all your ingredients together until you get a soft dough. If your dough is too wet or sticky, add a bit more of the cocoa powder.

2. Roll your dough into 8 truffles.

3. Pour some cocoa powder into a bowl and coat your truffles with it.

Nutritional data per truffle: 41 kcals, 3 grams protein, 3 grams carbs, and 2 grams fat

¼ cup pea protein powder

1 tablespoon granulated stevia (or your low-carb sweetener of choice)

2 squares (20 grams) dark chocolate (90%), melted

4 tablespoons almond milk

1 tablespoon agave, maple, or date syrup

2 tablespoons cocoa powder, plus more for coating

MACADAMIA ENERGY TRUFFLES

2 pitted medjool dates

¼ cup macadamia nuts

4 brazil nuts

1 tablespoon vanilla bean paste

1 teaspoon melted coconut oil

2 tablespoons pea protein powder

Whenever I get asked if I fear there's a day when I'll run out of recipe ideas, I shrug and say, hand on my heart, I don't think so. You see, I love food! And whenever I eat something that I think can be turned into a nutritious protein treat, I head to my kitchen and do it. Take, for example, these energy truffles. They were born out of my love for macadamia nut cookies!

MAKES 8 TRUFFLES

1. In a small food processor, mix all your ingredients together until you get a soft dough that you can shape with your hands. If your dough is too wet or sticky, add a bit more of the pea protein powder.

2. Roll your dough into 8 truffles.

Nutritional data per truffle: 62 kcals, 2 grams protein, 5 grams carbs, and 4 grams fat

COMPARED TO ALMONDS AND PEANUTS, MACADAMIA NUTS ARE LOWER IN PROTEIN AND MUCH HIGHER IN FAT. BUT DON'T LET THAT DISSUADE YOU FROM EATING THEM! MACADAMIA NUTS ARE PACKED FULL OF ANTIOXIDANTS, NUTRIENTS, AND HEALTHY MONOUNSATURATED FATTY ACIDS. THEY'RE ALSO CREAMY AND, IN MY OPINION AT LEAST, ABSOLUTELY DELICIOUS.

CHOCOLATE COCONUT ENERGY TRUFFLES

1–2 tablespoons freshly brewed espresso

½ cup gluten-free rolled oats

2 tablespoons whey protein powder

1 tablespoon cocoa powder

1 tablespoon granulated stevia (or your low-carb sweetener of choice

1 teaspoon vanilla extract

2 tablespoons coconut flakes

This recipe is my protein take on the Swedish confectionery *chokladboll*, a type of truffle made up of sugar, cocoa, oats, and butter that is bound with coffee and then rolled on coconut. It's an extremely tasty snack! But not exactly a health food. So I figured, hey, why don't we take the essence of chokladboll and create a delicious protein snack? That's how this recipe was born. Now, one thing you'll notice here is that I use freshly brewed espresso instead of milk to bind my ingredients together. Of course, if you don't like coffee, you can substitute almond milk or rice milk. But consider adding the coffee instead—it adds a subtle hint of espresso while helping to amplify the cocoa in the recipe.

MAKES 6 TRUFFLES

1. In a small food processor, combine all the ingredients, except the coconut flakes, until you get a soft dough. If your dough is too wet or sticky, add a bit more of the oats.

2. Roll your dough into 6 truffles.

3. Pour coconut flakes into a bowl and coat your truffles with it.

Nutritional data per truffle: 48 kcals, 3 grams protein, 5 grams carbs, and 2 grams fat

SPICE AND ALL THINGS NICE TRUFFLES

Last Christmas, a good friend of mine gave me a basket of holiday foods that included a bag of walnuts, some dates, a bunch of dried cranberries, dried apricots, and a big ol' slice of Christmas cake. I wasn't too excited by the cake (I've never liked Christmas cake), but the rest? Oh, the rest I was extremely happy with! Because I love Christmas flavors. You know, cinnamon, walnuts, and allspice? Delicious Christmasy snacks enjoyed with a cup of hot chocolate by an open fire with some thick socks on my feet? Yeah. Those are the feelings and flavors that inspired this recipe. Whether it's Christmas or the middle of summer, though, these treats will set your heart ablaze.

MAKES 16 TRUFFLES

1. Mix all your ingredients together in a small food processor until you get a dough that you can shape with your hands.

2. Roll this dough into 16 truffles.

Nutritional data per truffle: 56 kcals, 3 grams protein, 6 grams carbs, and 2 grams fat

3 pitted medjool dates

¼ cup pea protein powder

3 tablespoons pumpkin seeds

3 tablespoons hulled hemp seeds

4 tablespoons dried fruit (I use a combination of dried raisins, cranberries, and apricots)

3 tablespoons dried cranberries

3 teaspoons honey

1 tablespoon almond milk

1 handful walnuts

Pinch of cinnamon

Pinch of allspice

VANILLA ORANGE OATMEAL TRUFFLES

Truffles

¼ cup gluten-free rolled oats

2 tablespoons almond butter

¼ cup pea protein powder

2 tablespoons coconut sugar

1 tablespoon vanilla bean paste

Zest from ½ orange

3 tablespoons almond milk

2 tablespoons ground almonds

Coating

3 squares (30 grams) dark chocolate (70–90%)

1 teaspoon orange zest

This recipe was a mistake. In other words, it happened by chance. It was actually meant to be a recipe for flapjacks! But after I made the dough I realized, you know what? This dough is perfect for truffles. It's sweet, soft, and just delightful, especially covered in dark chocolate. So truffles the dough became—delicious protein truffles packed full of oaty goodness.

MAKES 8 TRUFFLES

1. In a small food processor, mix all the truffle ingredients together, until you get a soft dough that you can shape with your hands. If your dough is too wet or sticky, add a bit more of the ground almonds.

2. Roll your dough into 8 truffles.

3. Melt the dark chocolate in a bain-marie (i.e., a glass bowl on top of a pot of boiling water).

4. Using a spatula (or your hands), dip the truffles into the chocolate.

5. Place the chocolate-coated truffles onto a nonstick silicone tray or a tray covered with baking paper or aluminum foil. Top with the orange zest.

6. Leave in the fridge for a couple of hours until the chocolate sets or, if you're in a hurry, put them in the freezer for 20 to 30 minutes.

Nutritional data per truffle: 90 kcals, 5 grams protein, 5 grams carbs, and 5 grams fat

COCOA NIB COFFEE TRUFFLES

Whenever I host protein bar and truffle workshops, I bring cocoa nibs for people to experiment with. It always amazes me that most people have never actually tried cocoa nibs. What are cocoa nibs? They are the small pieces of cacao that chocolate producers end up with after drying, fermenting, roasting, and crushing the beans to make chocolate. You can find cocoa nibs in the baking aisle of most health-food stores. They look a bit like weirdly shaped pebbles. But don't let their appearance deceive you. Cocoa nibs are really good for you, extremely crunchy, and have a delicious cocoa liqueur flavor to them. They're more bitter than sweet, but they capture the essence of cacao beautifully and, when used in chocolate snacks and desserts, they add an extra dimension of cocoa **POW!**

MAKES 10 TRUFFLES

1. In a small food processor, combine all the ingredients, except for the dark chocolate and shaved white chocolate, until you get a soft dough that you can shape with your hands. If your mixture is too wet or sticky, add a bit more of the ground almonds.

2. Roll your dough into 10 truffles.

3. Melt the dark chocolate in a bain-marie (i.e., a glass bowl on top of a pot of boiling water). Using a spatula (or your hands), dip the truffles into the chocolate.

4. Place the chocolate-coated truffles onto a nonstick silicone tray or a tray covered with baking paper or aluminum foil. Top with a bit more of the cocoa nibs and some shaved white chocolate.

5. Leave in the fridge for a couple of hours until the chocolate sets or, if you're in a hurry, put them in the freezer for 20 to 30 minutes.

Nutritional data per truffle: 72 kcals, 2.8 grams protein, 2.5 grams carbs, and 6 grams fat

Truffles

2 tablespoons whey protein powder

2 tablespoons cocoa nibs

2 tablespoons coconut sugar (see note)

1 tablespoon cocoa powder

½ cup ground almonds

2–3 tablespoons freshly brewed espresso

2 tablespoons coconut flour

1 tablespoon cocoa nibs, plus more for coating

Coating

3 squares (30 grams) dark chocolate

1 teaspoon shaved white chocolate

Note: *If you want your truffles to be lower in carbs, use granulated stevia instead of coconut sugar.*

ALMOND CRANBERRY PROTEIN TRUFFLES

¼ cup gluten-free rolled oats

1–2 tablespoons agave, honey, or date syrup (depending on your sweetness preference)

¼ cup whey protein powder

¼ cup ground almonds

1 tablespoon almond milk

2 tablespoons coconut flour

1–2 tablespoons chopped dried cranberries (or dates or dried figs)

Cinnamon, to taste

I created these truffles for those of you who prefer chewy over soft and cookie-doughy truffles. These truffles are a lot more like the energy protein balls you see in supermarkets and health-food stores nowadays. They're denser than most of my truffles, which means that they're a lot easier to transport from your kitchen to the gym, office, school, or the great outdoors!

MAKES 8 TRUFFLES

1. In a small food processor, combine all your ingredients together, except for the cinnamon, until you get a soft dough that you can shape with your hands. If your mixture is too sticky or wet, add a tiny bit more of the ground almonds. If it's too dry, add a tiny bit more of the milk.

2. Roll your dough into 8 truffles.

3. Pour cinnamon into a bowl and coat your truffles with it.

Nutritional data per truffle: 65 kcals, 4 grams protein, 6 grams carbs, and 3 grams fat

YOU CAN ALSO COAT THESE TRUFFLES IN GROUND ALMONDS OR COCONUT FLAKES.

DARK CHOCOLATE AND ALMOND MANIA PROTEIN TRUFFLES

These truffles are soft, almost gooey, and they taste like . . . a combination of chocolate cookie dough and almond butter and extra chocolate. You have to make them to truly appreciate their simplicity and unbelievable moreishness!

MAKES 10 BIG TRUFFLES OR 20 SMALL ONES

1. In a medium-size bowl with a spatula, mix all the ingredients together, except for almond butter, until you get a soft dough that you can shape with your hands. If your mixture is too wet or sticky, add a bit more ground almonds and/or cocoa.

2. Roll your dough into ten big truffles (or twenty small ones).

3. Flatten each truffle into a cookie shape and add a dollop of almond butter in the middle of each before rolling them back into a ball again. This gives the truffles a delicious almond butter heart!

Nutritional data per truffle: 128 kcals, 7 grams protein, 4 grams carbs, and 9 grams fat

3 tablespoons coconut sugar (or granulated stevia if you want them to be lower in carbs)

1 cup ground almonds

¼ cup cocoa powder

¼ cup whey protein powder

4 tablespoons almond milk

2 tablespoons almond butter

HEMP COCOA DARK CHOCOLATE TRUFFLES

Truffles

1 tablespoon coconut flour

¼ cup hemp protein powder

2 tablespoons cocoa powder

2 tablespoons almond milk

2 tablespoons coconut sugar

¼ cup hulled hemp seeds, plus more for topping

¼ cup coconut flakes

Coating

5 squares (50 grams) dark chocolate (70-90%)

Like I said in the previous chapter, hemp protein powder is tricky to work with because it has an extremely strong, grassy flavor. So it doesn't work well in vanilla truffles or any kind of truffle that doesn't feature an extreme punch of cocoa or another very strong flavor. It doesn't mean that hemp protein powder is impossible to use, though. It just means that you have to treat it differently than you would pea or whey protein powder.

MAKES 8 TRUFFLES

1. In a small food processor, combine all the ingredients, except for the dark chocolate, until you get a soft dough that you can shape with your hands. If your mixture is too wet or sticky, add a bit more of the coconut flour or cocoa powder, if you want your truffles to be extra chocolatey.

2. Roll your dough into 8 truffles.

3. Melt the dark chocolate in a bain-marie (i.e., a glass bowl on top of a pot of boiling water).

4. Using a spatula (or your hands), dip the truffles into the chocolate.

5. Place the chocolate-coated truffles onto a nonstick silicone tray or a tray covered with baking paper or aluminum foil. Sprinkle extra hulled hemp seeds on top.

6. Leave in the fridge for a couple of hours until the chocolate sets or, if you're in a hurry, put them in the freezer for 20 to 30 minutes.

Nutritional data per truffle: 106 kcals, 5 grams protein, 6 grams carbs, and 7 grams fat

SUNFLOWER HONEY PROTEIN TRUFFLES

Many people ask me what the best substitute for almond or peanut butter is. My answer is always the same: sunflower seed butter, or tahini (a.k.a. sesame seed butter). They are both great subs for almond or peanut butter. Bear in mind that they are a lot stronger in flavor and a bit . . . savory. Including honey whenever you use a seed butter is such a good idea. The combination of honey and seeds is actually the basis of many delicious snacks and desserts, like these protein truffles.

MAKES 6 TRUFFLES

1. In a medium-size bowl with a spatula, mix all your ingredients together, except for the dark chocolate, until you get a soft dough that you can shape with your hands. If your mixture is too wet or sticky, add a bit more pea protein powder.

2. Roll your dough into 6 truffles.

3. Melt the dark chocolate in a bain-marie (i.e., a glass bowl on top of a pot of boiling water).

4. Using a spatula (or your hands), dip the truffles into the chocolate.

5. Place the chocolate-coated truffles onto a nonstick silicone tray or a tray covered with baking paper or aluminum foil.

6. Leave in the fridge for a couple of hours until the chocolate sets or, if you're in a hurry, put them in the freezer for 20 to 30 minutes.

Nutritional data per truffle (without the chocolate coating): 45 kcals, 4 grams protein, 4 grams carbs, and 1 gram fat

Truffles

¼ cup pea protein powder

1 tablespoon sunflower seed butter

½ tablespoon honey

1 tablespoon cashew milk

1 tablespoon vanilla extract

Coating

4 squares (40 grams) dark chocolate (70–90%)

COFFEE PROTEIN TRUFFLES

Truffles

2 tablespoons pea
protein powder

2 tablespoons cocoa
powder

4 tablespoons ground
almonds

1–2 teaspoons stevia
drops

2 tablespoons freshly
brewed coffee

2 tablespoons almond
milk

Coating

8 squares (80 grams)
dark chocolate (70–85%)

½ tablespoon grated
pistachio nuts, for
topping

I love making these bars and eating them pre-workout, alongside a large Americano. They're deeply chocolatey and the perfect companion to a cup of coffee for those days when you don't feel like eating a big breakfast but just want a bite of something quick before you hit the gym. Besides being delicious, they're also really pretty! So if you have a friend or family member that you think would love these, just stick a dozen inside a chocolate box and **POW!** You've got yourself a lovely present to give them.

MAKES 8 TRUFFLES

1. In a medium-size bowl with a spatula, mix all the ingredients together, except for the chocolate and grated pistachio nuts, until you get a soft dough that you can shape with your hands. If your mixture is too wet or sticky, add a bit more pea protein powder.

2. Roll your dough into 8 truffles.

3. Melt the dark chocolate in a bain-marie (i.e., a glass bowl on top of a pot of boiling water).

4. Using a spatula (or your hands), dip the truffles into the chocolate.

5. Place the chocolate-coated truffles onto a nonstick silicone tray or a tray covered with baking paper or aluminum foil. Sprinkle the truffles with the grated pistachios.

6. Leave in the fridge for a couple of hours until the chocolate sets or, if you're in a hurry, put them in the freezer for 20 to 30 minutes.

Nutritional data per truffle: 87 kcals, 4 grams protein, 3 grams carbs, and 7 grams fat

PROTEIN CHOCOLATE CUPS

Sunflower Honey
Protein Cups

Double Chocolate
Protein Cups

Chocolate Brownie Cups

Mini Peanut Butter
Protein Cups

Mini White Chocolate
Goji Cups

Orange Vanilla
Protein Cups

Chocolate cups are all the rage these days. They're convenient to carry and far more exciting to eat than a regular bar of chocolate because they contain secret fillings. It's a secret in that you can't see them when you unwrap your cup but then you bite in and **POW!** you get a delicious creamy center. What's not to love, right? I personally love making chocolate cups. They're quick, extremely easy, and you can fill them with all kinds of protein-packed doughs, nut butters, or pastes.

To make chocolate cups, protein-based or otherwise, all you need besides your ingredients are muffin cups—paper cups or silicone cups. You can also use little truffle cups to make bite-size chocolate cups, such as the ones on pages 111, 114, and 117. They're a fun variation and a great snack to have around when all you want is a bite of something sweet and delicious.

The way you make chocolate cups is simple: First, you make a dough, or filling. This can be any flavor you want and as doughy or pasty as you want. Then, you melt the chocolate (white, milk, or dark). After that, all you have to do is layer everything inside your cups. You start with the melted chocolate to cover the bottom and side of each cup. Then you add your dough in the middle and, finally, the rest of the melted chocolate. You then place the cups in the fridge for an hour or the freezer for 30 minutes and presto: You have your very own chocolate cups!

MINI PEANUT BUTTER PROTEIN CUPS

After you make these protein cups, consider wrapping each one individually in foil to eat whenever you feel like having a little delicious treat. The act of unwrapping, I'm convinced, makes things seem even more exciting! And these little cups are amazing enjoyed individually, as a post-dinner finisher, or simply as a snack when you crave a bite of something sweet that isn't insanely calorific.

MAKES 10 CUPS

1. In a medium-size bowl with a spatula, combine all the ingredients, except for the dark chocolate, until you get a soft dough that you can shape with your hands. If your mixture is too wet or sticky, add a bit more whey protein powder.

2. Divide the dough into ten marble-size balls and flatten each into the shape of a coin.

3. Get out 10 truffle-size paper cups.

4. Melt the dark chocolate in a bain-marie (i.e., a glass bowl on top of a pot of boiling water).

5. Cover half of the cups with the melted dark chocolate, add your dough, and cover the rest with dark chocolate.

6. Leave in the fridge for a couple of hours until the chocolate sets or, if you're in a hurry, put them in the freezer for 20 to 30 minutes.

Nutritional data per cup: 75 kcals, 3 grams protein, 2 grams carbs, and 6 grams fat

Cups

3 tablespoons chunky peanut butter

1 tablespoon almond milk

½ teaspoon vanilla bean paste

2 tablespoons whey protein powder

Coating

8 squares (80 grams) dark chocolate (70–80%)

ORANGE VANILLA PROTEIN CUPS

The dough inside these chocolate cups is delicious. It's a sweet vanilla, orange, and almond sensation! If you like the chocolate orange combination, you're in for a massive treat!

MAKES 5 CUPS

1. In a medium-size bowl with a spatula, combine all the ingredients, except for the dark chocolate, until you get a soft dough that you can shape with your hands. If your mixture is too wet or sticky, add a bit more whey protein powder.

2. Divide the dough into five marble-size balls and flatten each into the shape of a coin.

3. Get out 5 paper or silicone muffin cups.

4. Melt the dark chocolate in a bain-marie (i.e., a glass bowl on top of a pot of boiling water).

5. Cover half of the cups with the melted dark chocolate, add your dough, and cover the rest with dark chocolate.

6. Leave in the fridge for a couple of hours until the chocolate sets or, if you're in a hurry, put them in the freezer for 20 to 30 minutes.

Nutritional data per cup: 174 kcals, 9 grams protein, 5 grams carbs, and 12 grams fat

Cups

4 heaping tablespoons almond butter

¼ cup whey protein powder

1-2 teaspoons vanilla extract

1-2 teaspoons stevia drops, to taste

1 teaspoon orange zest

Coating

6 squares (60 grams) dark chocolate (70-80%)

DOUBLE CHOCOLATE PROTEIN CUPS

Cups

2 tablespoons pea protein powder

1 tablespoon cocoa powder

½ teaspoon stevia drops

2 tablespoons almond milk

1 tablespoon freshly brewed coffee

Coating

8 squares (80 grams) dark chocolate (70-90%)

These chocolate cups are different from most in that their filling doesn't include nut butter, so they're doughier. Creamier and softer too. More like . . . cake batter inside of a chocolate cup!

MAKES 10 CUPS

1. In a medium-size bowl with a spatula, combine all the ingredients, except for the dark chocolate, until you get a soft dough that you can shape with your hands. If your mixture is too wet or sticky, add a bit more pea protein powder.

2. Divide the dough into 10 marble-size balls and flatten each into the shape of a coin.

3. Get out 10 small truffle-size paper cups.

4. Melt the dark chocolate in a bain-marie (i.e., a glass bowl on top of a pot of boiling water).

5. Cover half of the cups with the melted dark chocolate, add your dough, and cover the rest with dark chocolate.

6. Leave in the fridge for a couple of hours until the chocolate sets or, if you're in a hurry, put them in the freezer for 20 to 30 minutes.

Nutritional data per cup: 50 kcals, 2 grams protein, 2 grams carbs, and 4 grams fat

MINI WHITE CHOCOLATE GOJI CUPS

These little cups are unlike anything I've ever made. They're crunchy, sweet, and packed full of flavor! They're the kind of thing I strongly urge you to make for a loved one if you want to collect points. They'll love you forever! Unless . . . unless you give them a box of these and proceed to eat them yourself. Look, it can happen . . . be warned: They're THAT good.

MAKES 10 CUPS

1. In a medium-size bowl with a spatula, combine all the ingredients, except for the white chocolate, until you get a soft dough that you can shape with your hands. If your dough is too dry and crumbly, add a bit more of the milk—be sure to start off with only a couple of extra teaspoons. You don't want to add too much liquid.

2. Divide the dough into 10 marble-size balls and flatten each into the shape of a coin.

3. Get out 10 small truffle-sized paper cups.

4. Melt the dark chocolate in a bain-marie (i.e., a glass bowl on top of a pot of boiling water).

5. Cover half of the cups with the melted dark chocolate, add your dough, and cover the rest with dark chocolate.

6. Leave in the fridge for a couple of hours until the chocolate sets or, if you're in a hurry, put them in the freezer for 20 to 30 minutes.

Nutritional data per cup: 79 kcals, 3 grams protein, 7 grams carbs, and 6 grams fat

Cups

4 tablespoons goji berries

2 tablespoons whey protein powder

1 tablespoon coconut flour

5 tablespoons flaked coconut

1 tablespoon almond milk

1 tablespoon cashew butter

1/2 teaspoon stevia drops (or your low-carb sweetener of choice)

Coating

6 squares (60 grams) sugar-free (or regular) white chocolate

SUNFLOWER HONEY PROTEIN CUPS

Cups

2 tablespoons sunflower butter

2 tablespoons honey or date syrup

2 tablespoons pea protein powder

Coating

5 squares (50 grams) dark chocolate

Like the Sunflower Honey Protein Truffles on page 105, these little cups combine sunflower seed butter and honey. What happens if you don't have sunflower seed butter? Well . . . you could use peanut or almond butter instead. Obviously your cups will be different from these but they'll be just as good!

MAKES 3 CUPS

1. In a medium-size bowl with a spatula, combine all the ingredients, except for the chocolate, until you get a dough that you can shape with your hands. If your dough is too crumbly, consider adding a bit of almond milk (add ½ teaspoon at a time, as you don't want too soft or too liquidy a dough).

2. Divide the dough into 3 marble-size balls and flatten each into the shape of a coin.

3. Get out 3 paper or silicone muffin cups.

4. Melt the dark chocolate in a bain-marie (i.e., a glass bowl on top of a pot of boiling water).

5. Cover half of the cups with the melted dark chocolate, add your dough, and cover the rest with dark chocolate.

6. Leave in the fridge for a couple of hours until the chocolate sets or, if you're in a hurry, put them in the freezer for 20 to 30 minutes.

Nutritional data per cup: 218 kcals, 9 grams protein, 10 grams carbs, and 16 grams fat

CHOCOLATE BROWNIE CUPS

This is a bit of a unusual recipe because in order to make it, you first have to make my Brownie Mug Cakes (page 182). I was debating whether to include it in this chapter since it's so atypical, but I decided I needed to because, while it is indeed different, it is out-of-this-world delicious! So it needs its own page, right here, among fellow chocolate cups.

MAKES 5 CUPS

1. Make the Brownie Mug Cakes.

2. Allow it to cool properly and dig in with a spoon to divide your brownies into five pieces of dough that you can roll with your hands into a ball and flatten into a muffin cup.

3. Melt the dark chocolate in a bain-marie (i.e., a glass bowl on top of a pot of boiling water).

4. Cover half of the cups with the melted dark chocolate, add your brownie dough, and cover the rest with dark chocolate.

5. Leave in the fridge for a couple of hours until the chocolate sets or, if you're in a hurry, put them in the freezer for 20 to 30 minutes.

Nutritional data per cup: 137 kcals, 5 grams protein, 11 grams carbs, and 8 grams fat

Cups

1 batch Brownie Mug Cakes (page 182)

Coating

7 squares (70 grams) dark chocolate

THIS IS ONE OF MY FAVORITE RECIPES IN THIS BOOK! IT'S CHOCOLATE ON CHOCOLATE ON CHOCOLATE—AN ABSOLUTE SENSATION FOR ANYONE WHO, LIKE ME, CONSIDERS THEMSELVES A DARK CHOCOLATE FIEND!

PROTEIN PANCAKES

Sweet Potato Pancakes

Banana Whey Protein Pancakes

Buttermilk Protein Pancakes

Spinach Protein Pancakes

Chocolate Protein Pancakes

Carrot Cake Protein Pancakes

Banana Nut Protein Pancakes

Butternut Squash Pancakes

Almond and Banana Protein Pancakes

Cranberry and Blueberry Protein Pancakes

Melon Pancakes

Apple and White Chocolate Protein Pancakes

Ricotta Whey Protein Pancakes

Flaxseed Protein Pancakes

Macadamia Nut Pancakes

Vegan Banana Pancakes

Vegan Crepe-Style Pancakes

Maple and Flax Protein Pancakes

Dairy-Free Protein Pancakes

Orange Sweet Potato Pancakes

I can't tell you the number of times people have gotten in touch to tell me that their protein batter "doesn't work" and/or that their pancakes have ended up stuck all over the pan and look more like scrambled pancakes than actual pancakes. What's wrong, they ask, with the batter? There's usually nothing wrong with the batter. The batter isn't a problem. You know what the problem is? The pan.

If you're serious about pancakes, buy a good nonstick pan or, better yet, a crepe or pancake pan. They're not at all expensive and they're critical when it comes to making a good stack of pancakes, protein-based or otherwise. Also, remember to always add either a bit of coconut oil or some low-calorie cooking spray to your pan before you make pancakes. No matter how nonstick your pan claims to be, a bit of oil will ensure that your pancakes glide off the pan and don't stick. You need this to be the case. Otherwise, next time you want to impress your loved one with your pancake-flipping skills, you'll end up standing there just shaking the pan like a buffoon, or worse, with pancake mush all over the ceiling and yourself.

I always add coconut oil to my pan when I make protein pancakes. I prefer it to low-calorie cookie spray, canola oil, or butter because it lends a wonderfully nutty taste to pancakes! If you're worried about calories and fat (because let's face it, coconut oil isn't exactly a light option), don't worry too much. You don't need much coconut oil to coat the bottom of your pan. A third of a teaspoon is enough to cover the whole surface and ensure that your pancakes don't stick.

SWEET POTATO PANCAKES

Most people make protein pancakes using bananas and that's fine—bananas are a great way to add moisture, sweetness, and flavor to protein pancakes. But you know what other ingredient can do exactly that? Sweet potatoes! They make pancakes extra fluffy and add a gorgeous sweetness to them too. Before you add them to your pancake batter, all you need to do is bake them until they're soft. I normally bake a huge bag of sweet potatoes every Sunday to enjoy during the week with some almond butter on top, as a veggie side to my lunch or dinner, or to use for protein pancakes!

MAKES 7 MEDIUM PANCAKES

1. Using a handheld immersion blender (or a small food processor), blend together all ingredients, except for the coconut oil, until you get a smooth batter.

2. Add a teaspoon of coconut oil or non-calorie cooking spray to a nonstick pan and heat the pan on high.

3. Pour your pancake batter on the pan and immediately turn down the heat to medium-low.

4. Flip the pancakes as soon as bubbles begin to form on the surface.

5. Repeat cooking steps for the rest of the batter.

6. Serve with your topping of choice.

Nutritional data per pancake: 105 kcals, 9 grams protein, 11 grams carbs, and 3 grams fat

1 large egg

1 large sweet potato, pre-baked

½ cup ground gluten-free oats

2 tablespoons vanilla extract

¼ cup whey protein powder

¼ cup almond flour

5 tablespoons almond milk

Coconut oil or non-calorie cooking spray, for the pan

BANANA WHEY PROTEIN PANCAKES

¼ cup whey protein powder

2 tablespoons coconut flour

1 medium banana

1 large egg

1 teaspoon vanilla extract

Coconut oil or non-calorie cooking spray, for the pan

I've been making these pancakes for years. They're really simple and a great post-workout meal! Top them with maple syrup, low-carb pancake syrup, bananas, or peanut/almond butter. They're a classic Protein Pow recipe and one that, if your taste buds are anything like mine, you're bound to make over and over again.

MAKES 3 MEDIUM PANCAKES

1. Using a handheld immersion blender (or a small food processor), blend together all the ingredients, except for the coconut oil, until you get a smooth batter.

2. Add a teaspoon of coconut oil or non-calorie cooking spray to a nonstick pan and heat the pan on high.

3. Pour your pancake batter on the pan and immediately turn down the heat to medium-low.

4. Flip the pancakes as soon as bubbles begin to form on the surface.

5. Repeat cooking steps for the rest of the batter.

6. Serve with your topping of choice.

Nutritional data per pancake: 108 kcals, 11 grams protein, 12 grams carbs, and 3 grams fat

BUTTERMILK PROTEIN PANCAKES

These pancakes are the closest to restaurant-style pancakes that you'll find in this book. After you add the syrup, bacon, and/or your topping of choice, they taste like something straight off a restaurant's breakfast menu! Give them a try—they're fluffy, soft, and perfect with a bit of butter and some good ol' fashioned maple syrup!

MAKES 4 MEDIUM PANCAKES

1. Using a handheld immersion blender (or a small food processor), blend together all ingredients, except for the coconut oil, until you get a smooth batter.

2. Add a teaspoon of coconut oil or non-calorie cooking spray to a nonstick pan and heat the pan on high.

3. Pour your pancake batter on the pan and immediately turn down the heat to medium-low.

4. Flip the pancakes as soon as bubbles begin to form on the surface.

5. Repeat cooking steps for the rest of the batter.

6. Serve with your topping of choice.

Nutrition data for 4 pancakes: 258 kcals, 34 grams protein, 20 grams carbs, and 5 grams fat

1 fresh large egg white

¼ cup almond milk (regular milk would work, too)

2 tablespoons ground gluten-free oats

½ tablespoon pea protein powder

¼ cup whey protein powder

2 tablespoons buttermilk powder

½ teaspoon baking powder

½ tablespoon vanilla extract

Coconut oil or non-calorie cooking spray, for the pan

SPINACH PROTEIN PANCAKES

2 large eggs

½ cup gluten-free rolled oats

¼ cup whey protein

1 medium banana

¼ cup ground almonds

1 handful fresh spinach

Coconut oil or non-calorie cooking spray, for the pan

When you make these pancakes, your batter will look a bit like mushy baby food. Don't despair. Just get a good quality non-stick pan out, add some coconut oil or low-calorie cooking spray to it, and pour your batter in the middle of the pan, spreading it around with a spoon so it becomes thinner. Turn the heat down to medium-low and wait until the bottom of the pancake has cooked through. Then flip, cook on the other side, and **POW!** your Popeye pancakes are ready to serve.

MAKES 4 LARGE PANCAKES

1. Using a handheld immersion blender (or a small food processor), blend together all ingredients, except for the coconut oil, until you get a smooth batter.

2. Add a teaspoon of coconut oil or non-calorie cooking spray to a nonstick pan and heat the pan on high.

3. Pour your pancake batter on the pan and immediately turn down the heat to medium-low.

4. Flip the pancakes as soon as bubbles begin to form on the surface.

5. Repeat cooking steps for the rest of the batter.

6. Serve with your topping of choice.

Nutrition data for 4 pancakes: 590 kcals, 42 grams protein, 47 grams carbs, 27 grams fat

CHOCOLATE PROTEIN PANCAKES

Chocolate pancakes aren't as common as vanilla or banana ones, but they're just as good. I made these pancakes as an experiment one day, post-workout. I wasn't sure whether they'd work—I don't often make chocolate pancakes. But they did! And since then I've been making them a lot. They're a good change of pace from my other pancakes, a nice variation for when you feel like having something a bit different.

MAKES 4 MEDIUM PANCAKES

1. Using a handheld immersion blender (or a small food processor), blend together all the ingredients, except for the coconut oil, until you get a smooth batter.

2. Add a teaspoon of coconut oil or non-calorie cooking spray to a nonstick pan and heat the pan on high.

3. Pour your pancake batter on the pan and immediately turn down the heat to medium-low.

4. Flip the pancakes as soon as bubbles begin to form on the surface.

5. Repeat cooking steps for second half of the batter.

6. Serve with your topping of choice.

Nutritional data for 4 pancakes: 302 kcals, 18 grams protein, 42 grams carbs, and 7 grams fat

3 fresh large egg whites

¼ cup whey protein powder

1 tablespoon cocoa powder

1 medium banana

4 tablespoons gluten-free self-rising flour

2 tablespoons almond milk

2 tablespoons ground almonds

Coconut oil or non-calorie cooking spray, for the pan

CARROT CAKE PROTEIN PANCAKES

½ cup gluten-free rolled oats

1 large fresh egg white

2 tablespoons chopped walnuts and/or almonds

2 tablespoons whey protein powder

2 tablespoons coconut sugar (or your low-carb sweetener of choice)

2 tablespoons almond milk

½ teaspoon cinnamon

1 teaspoon vanilla bean paste

2 small carrots, grated

Coconut oil or non-calorie cooking spray, for the pan

You may notice, in this chapter, that I call for you to make either big or small pancakes with your batters. That's because when you have a thick batter, such as this one for carrot cake pancakes, making small pancakes is best. They're much easier to flip when they're small and, by making them small, you can also get away with having them be thicker.

MAKES 4 SMALL PANCAKES

1. Using a handheld immersion blender (or a small food processor), blend together all the ingredients, except for the carrots and coconut oil, until you get a smooth batter.

2. Squeeze out any excess water from the grated carrots with a paper towel. Add the grated carrots to the batter.

3. Add a teaspoon of coconut oil or non-calorie cooking spray to a nonstick pan and heat the pan to high.

4. Pour your pancake batter on the pan and immediately turn down the heat to medium-low.

5. Flip the pancakes as soon as bubbles begin to form on the surface.

6. Repeat cooking steps for the rest of the batter.

7. Serve with your topping of choice.

Nutritional data for 4 pancakes: 478 kcals, 37 grams protein, 50 grams carbs, and 13 grams fat

BANANA NUT PROTEIN PANCAKES

This recipe was inspired by my unwavering love for banana nut bread. Like the Carrot Cake Protein Pancakes on page 134, these pancakes are thick, moist, and delicious! Almost like dessert, these are the perfect stack to enjoy after a long workout!

MAKES 5 SMALL PANCAKES

1. Using a handheld immersion blender (or a small food processor), blend together all the ingredients, except for the coconut oil, until you get a light and fluffy batter.

2. Add a teaspoon of coconut oil or non-calorie cooking spray to a nonstick pan and heat the pan to high.

3. Pour your pancake batter on the pan and immediately turn down the heat to medium-low.

4. Flip the pancakes as soon as bubbles begin to form on the surface.

5. Repeat cooking steps for the rest of the batter.

6. Serve with your topping of choice.

Nutritional data for 5 pancakes: 260 kcals, 21 grams protein, 31 grams carbs, and 7 grams fat

2 large fresh egg whites

1 medium banana

2 tablespoons pea protein powder

½ tablespoon vanilla bean paste

1 tablespoon chopped walnuts

½ teaspoon cinnamon

Coconut oil or non-calorie cooking spray, for the pan

BUTTERNUT SQUASH PANCAKES

½ cup steamed (or baked) butternut squash

1 large whole egg, plus 2 large egg whites

¼ cup whey protein powder

2 tablespoons coconut flour

Coconut oil or non-calorie cooking spray, for the pan

Butternut squash is a great substitute for sweet potatoes, which are a great substitute for bananas, in protein pancakes. They ensure that your batter doesn't end up dry and your pancakes never come out rubbery like a lot of whey protein-based pancakes tend to do! If you don't have butternut squash around, or you want to play around with this recipe, you can use pumpkin too. Just be sure, if you do that, to steam it until it softens before adding it to your batter.

MAKES 3 MEDIUM PANCAKES

1. Using a handheld immersion blender (or a small food processor), blend together all the ingredients, except for the coconut oil, until you get a smooth batter.

2. Add a teaspoon of coconut oil or non-calorie cooking spray to a nonstick pan and heat the pan to high.

3. Pour your pancake batter on the pan and immediately turn down the heat to medium-low.

4. Flip the pancakes as soon as bubbles begin to form on the surface.

5. Repeat cooking steps for the rest of the batter.

6. Serve with your topping of choice.

Nutritional data for 3 pancakes: 325 kcals, 38 grams protein, 28 grams carbs, and 7 grams fat

ALMOND AND BANANA PROTEIN PANCAKES

Do you ever peel a banana, look at it, and think, "I need something with you," so you open your cupboard, take out your almond or peanut butter, and scoop some of it to put on the banana? I do. All the time. And that's what inspired this recipe: a love for bananas and almonds. A match made in heaven, if you ask me! Topped with almond butter, these pancakes are seriously amazing. Give them a shot and you'll see.

2 medium bananas

¼ cup whey protein powder

2 large whole eggs

⅓ cup ground almonds

Coconut oil or non-calorie cooking spray, for the pan

MAKES 6 SMALL PANCAKES

1. Using a handheld immersion blender (or a small food processor), blend together all the ingredients, except for the coconut oil, until you get a smooth and fluffy batter.

2. Add a teaspoon of coconut oil or non-calorie cooking spray to a nonstick pan and heat the pan to high.

3. Pour your pancake batter on the pan and immediately turn down the heat to medium-low.

4. Flip the pancakes as soon as bubbles begin to form on the surface.

5. Repeat cooking steps for the rest of the batter.

6. Serve with your topping of choice.

Nutritional data for 3 pancakes: 284 kcals, 19 grams protein, 27 grams carbs, and 13 grams fat

CRANBERRY AND BLUEBERRY PROTEIN PANCAKES

My dad is obsessed with berries. I'm always in awe of how many berries the man can eat. He eats blueberries and cherries like it's his job and for Thanksgiving and Christmas every year, he consumes an absolutely ludicrous amount of cranberry sauce! So when he came to visit us last month, I knew I'd have to make him some kind of delicious berry-themed pancakes. Needless to say, he ate them all—with blueberries on the side and dried cranberries on top.

MAKES 4 MEDIUM PANCAKES

1. Using a handheld immersion blender (or a small food processor), blend together all the ingredients, except for the coconut oil, until you get a smooth and fluffy batter.

2. Add a teaspoon of coconut oil or non-calorie cooking spray to a nonstick pan and heat the pan to high.

3. Pour your pancake batter on the pan and immediately turn down the heat to medium-low.

4. Flip the pancakes as soon as bubbles begin to form on the surface.

5. Repeat cooking steps for the rest of the batter.

6. Top with cranberries and blueberries.

Nutritional data for 4 pancakes: 280 kcals, 17 grams protein, 45 grams carbs, and 2 grams fat

2 tablespoons whey protein powder

1 large fresh egg white

¼ cup gluten-free rolled oats

1 tablespoon cranberries (or goji berries), plus more for topping

1 handful fresh blueberries, plus more for topping

1 pitted medjool date, chopped

Coconut oil or non-calorie cooking spray, for the pan

MELON PANCAKES

¾ cup chopped fresh cantaloupe

3 large fresh egg whites

½ cup gluten-free rolled oats

2 tablespoons coconut flour

¼ cup whey protein powder

½ teaspoon stevia drops

Coconut oil or non-calorie cooking spray, for the pan

It may sound weird to you: melon in pancakes!? But trust me, it works. Melon adds a subtle sweetness to the pancakes while making them extra moist and delicious. It's actually great in baking too. If you happen not to have any melon around, though, or if you're just not a big fan of melon, don't worry. You can substitute applesauce for the melon in this recipe and still end up with gorgeous pancakes.

MAKES 4 SMALL PANCAKES

1. Using a handheld immersion blender (or a small food processor), blend together all of ingredients, except for the coconut oil, until you get a smooth and fluffy batter.

2. Add a teaspoon of coconut oil or non-calorie cooking spray to a nonstick pan and heat the pan to high.

3. Pour your pancake batter on the pan and immediately turn down the heat to medium-low.

4. Flip the pancakes as soon as bubbles begin to form on the surface.

5. Repeat cooking steps for the rest of the batter.

6. Serve with your topping of choice.

Nutritional data for 2 pancakes: 270 kcals, 24 grams protein, 23 grams carbs, and 19 grams fat

APPLE AND WHITE CHOCOLATE PROTEIN PANCAKES

By now you may have noticed a theme running through all my protein pancake recipes: most of them contain fruits and/or vegetables. I love adding them to my batters. Fruits and vegetables make pancakes ever more nutritious, tasty, and moist. They're less prone to get dry and rubbery. Topped with maple syrup or low-carb pancake syrup, these pancakes are absolutely amazing!

MAKES 4 LARGE PANCAKES

1. Using a handheld immersion blender (or a small food processor), blend together all the ingredients, except for the white chocolate chips and coconut oil, until you get a smooth and fluffy batter. Once blended, add the white chocolate chips.

2. Add a teaspoon of coconut oil or non-calorie cooking spray to a nonstick pan and heat the pan to high.

3. Pour your pancake batter on the pan and immediately turn down the heat to medium-low.

4. Flip the pancakes as soon as bubbles begin to form on the surface.

5. Repeat cooking steps for the rest of the batter.

6. Serve with your topping of choice.

Nutritional data for 2 pancakes: 212 kcals, 21 grams protein, 24 grams carbs, and 4 grams fat

4 large fresh egg whites

½ cup gluten-free rolled oats

1 apple, cored and chopped into small pieces

¼ cup whey protein powder

2 teaspoons vanilla bean paste

1 tablespoon sugar-free or regular white chocolate chips

Coconut oil or non-calorie cooking spray, for the pan

RICOTTA WHEY PROTEIN PANCAKES

When I made these pancakes, I couldn't stop looking at them. They are . . . perfect. I took close to fifty photos of them. They're the kind of pancakes that you'd gladly print on an ad; the kind of fluffy pancakes you want to jump into; the kind of pancakes that you just want to devour.

MAKES 10 SMALL PANCAKES

1. Using a handheld immersion blender (or a small food processor), blend together all the ingredients, except for the coconut oil, until you get a smooth batter.

2. Add a teaspoon of coconut oil or non-calorie cooking spray to a nonstick pan and heat the pan to high.

3. Pour your pancake batter on the pan and immediately turn down the heat to medium-low.

4. Flip the pancakes as soon as bubbles begin to form on the surface.

5. Repeat cooking steps for the rest of the batter.

6. Serve with your topping of choice.

Nutritional data for 5 pancakes: 164 kcals, 21 grams protein, 17 grams carbs, and 3 grams fat

3 large fresh egg whites

2 tablespoons almond milk

¼ cup low-fat ricotta cheese

2 tablespoons whey protein powder

2 tablespoons brown rice flour

2 tablespoons coconut flour

Coconut oil or non-calorie cooking spray, for the pan

FLAXSEED PROTEIN PANCAKES

2 tablespoons pea protein powder

4 tablespoons almond milk

2 large fresh egg whites

1 teaspoon vanilla bean paste

3 tablespoons ground flaxseed

Coconut oil or non-calorie cooking spray, for the pan

Flaxseed is one of those foods that everyone is always urging you to eat more of. I normally have a giant bag in the fridge and I go through it pretty quickly by adding it to salads, oats, and even chicken dishes. I also use flaxseed in pancakes. It makes them taste nutty and almost wholemeal-y and adds a heap-ton of fiber.

MAKES 4 MEDIUM PANCAKES

1. Using a handheld immersion blender (or a small food processor), blend together all the ingredients, except for the coconut oil, until you get a smooth batter.

2. Add a teaspoon of coconut oil or non-calorie cooking spray to a nonstick pan and heat the pan to high.

3. Pour your pancake batter on the pan and immediately turn down the heat to medium-low.

4. Flip the pancakes as soon as bubbles begin to form on the surface.

5. Repeat cooking steps for the rest of the batter.

6. Serve with your topping of choice.

Nutritional data for 4 pancakes: 287 kcals, 26 grams protein, 3 grams carbs, and 16 grams fat

MACADAMIA NUT PANCAKES

Macadamia nuts are a bit of an underdog nut—no one talks about them much. I did a simple Internet search the other day. Guess how many times people posted about peanuts? 87.3 million times. Almonds? 61.4 million times. Macadamia nuts, on the other hand? A sad 403,000 times. I guess it's not surprising: They're a lot more expensive, higher in calories and fat, and lower in protein. They're also harder to turn into nut butter because they're so fatty. But you know what? They're my favorite nut. They're just so unique and nutty and they taste a bit creamy, too. If you're a fan of macadamia nuts, you've got to try this recipe. It's one of my favorites in this book!

MAKES 3 MEDIUM PANCAKES

3 large fresh egg whites

¼ cup pea protein powder

6 tablespoons almond milk

¼ cup gluten-free rolled oats

¼ cup macadamia nuts

1 tablespoon vanilla bean paste

Coconut oil or non-calorie cooking spray, for the pan

1. Using a handheld immersion blender (or a small food processor), blend together all the ingredients, except for the coconut oil, until you get a smooth batter.

2. Add a teaspoon of coconut oil or non-calorie cooking spray to a nonstick pan and heat the pan to high.

3. Pour your pancake batter on the pan and immediately turn down the heat to medium-low.

4. Flip the pancakes as soon as bubbles begin to form on the surface.

5. Repeat cooking steps for the rest of the batter.

6. Serve with your topping of choice.

Nutritional data for 3 pancakes: 458 kcals, 38 grams protein, 18 grams carbs, and 26 grams fat

VEGAN BANANA PANCAKES

¼ cup gluten-free rolled oats

1 tablespoon almond milk

2 tablespoons pea protein powder

1 medium banana

1 tablespoon smooth peanut butter

2 tablespoons blueberries

Coconut oil or non-calorie cooking spray, for the pan

When you make these pancakes, please make them small because they're mushy and impossible to flip if you make them too big. That doesn't mean they're not good though—they are! They're soft, delicious, and a wonderful alternative for those of you who don't eat eggs or dairy.

MAKES 3 SMALL PANCAKES

1. Using a handheld immersion blender (or a small food processor), blend together all the ingredients, except for the blueberries and coconut oil, until you get a smooth thick batter. Add the blueberries to the batter.

2. Add a teaspoon of coconut oil or non-calorie cooking spray to a nonstick pan and heat the pan to high.

3. Pour your pancake batter on the pan and immediately turn down the heat to medium-low.

4. Flip the pancakes as soon as bubbles begin to form on the surface.

5. Repeat cooking steps for the rest of the batter.

6. Serve with your topping of choice.

Nutritional data for 3 pancakes: 329 kcals, 20 grams protein, 42 grams carbs, and 8 grams fat

VEGAN CREPE-STYLE PANCAKES

Unlike the previous recipe, these pancakes are best if you make them large. The batter is just a lot thinner and works better if you spread it on the entire surface of your pan before flipping. Once your pancake is done, feel free to eat it rolled up or fill it with nut butter and/or fruit before adding maple syrup or your low-carb syrup of choice of top.

MAKES 2 LARGE PANCAKES

1. Using a handheld immersion blender (or a small food processor), blend together all the ingredients, except for the coconut oil, until you get a smooth thick batter.

2. Add a teaspoon of coconut oil or non-calorie cooking spray to a nonstick pan and heat the pan to high.

3. With a spoon, spread half of the batter until it covers the entire surface of the pan. Immediately turn down the heat to medium-low.

4. Flip the pancakes as soon as bubbles begin to form on the surface.

5. Repeat cooking steps for the other half of the batter.

6. Serve with your topping of choice.

Nutritional data per pancake: 179 kcals, 14 grams protein, 27 grams carbs, and 1 gram fat

¼ cup pea protein powder

14 tablespoons almond milk

1 tablespoon vanilla bean paste

½ cup self-raising gluten-free flour

Coconut oil or non-calorie cooking spray, for the pan

CONSIDER ADDING SOME BANANA SLICES AND A BIT OF PEANUT OR ALMOND BUTTER ON TOP OF THESE CREPES! OR, IF YOU WANT TO GO A DIFFERENT ROUTE, ADD SOME CARAMELIZED ORANGES AND CINNAMON ON TOP.

MAPLE AND FLAX PROTEIN PANCAKES

2 tablespoons flaxseed

3 pitted medjool dates, chopped

½ cup gluten-free rolled oats

¼ cup whey protein powder

½ cup liquid egg whites

2 tablespoons almond milk

1 teaspoon natural maple flavoring or vanilla extract (optional)

Coconut oil or non-calorie cooking spray, for the pan

As with the Flaxseed Protein Pancakes (page 148), this recipe uses flaxseed to add fiber as well as a delicious nutty flavor to the pancakes. Note here that I use natural maple flavoring—you don't have to use it if you can't find it. A friend of mine gave me a little bottle and it's really nice to add to pancake batters! There are a few companies that sell it online but, again, if you don't have it or don't want to get it, go without it or use vanilla extract instead.

MAKES 7 SMALL PANCAKES

1. Using a handheld immersion blender (or a small food processor), blend together all the ingredients, except for the coconut oil, until you get a smooth thick batter.

2. Add a teaspoon of coconut oil or non-calorie cooking spray to a nonstick pan and heat the pan to high.

3. Spoon your pancake batter on the pan and immediately turn down the heat to medium-low.

4. Flip the pancakes as soon as bubbles begin to form on the surface.

5. Repeat cooking steps for the rest of the batter.

6. Serve with your topping of choice.

Nutritional data for 3 pancakes: 323 kcals, 24 grams protein, 45 grams carbs, and 7 grams fat

DAIRY-FREE PROTEIN PANCAKES

In this recipe, I made 7 little pancakes. You don't have to make them as small if you don't want to. I just like to stack my pancakes as high as possible! But if you're not into such shenanigans, feel free to make 3 or 4 medium pancakes! It's up to you and how high you want to stack them, hehe.

MAKES 7 SMALL PANCAKES

1. Using a handheld immersion blender (or a small food processor), blend together all the ingredients, except for the coconut oil, until you get a smooth thick batter.

2. Add a teaspoon of coconut oil or non-calorie cooking spray to a nonstick pan and heat the pan to high.

3. Spoon your pancake batter on the pan and immediately turn down the heat to medium-low.

4. Flip the pancakes as soon as bubbles begin to form on their surface.

5. Repeat cooking steps for the rest of the batter.

6. Serve with your topping of choice.

Nutritional data for 7 pancakes: 331 kcals, 19 grams protein, 45 grams carbs, and 9 grams fat

¼ cup gluten-free rolled oats

2 tablespoons pea protein powder

½ teaspoon stevia drops

1 large whole egg

4 tablespoons cashew milk

1 medium banana

1 tablespoon smooth peanut butter

1 teaspoon vanilla bean paste

Coconut oil or non-calorie cooking spray, for the pan

ORANGE SWEET POTATO PANCAKES

3 large fresh egg whites

¼ cup whey protein powder

½ large sweet potato, pre-baked

¼ cup of ground almonds

1 tablespoon pea protein powder

½ tablespoon orange zest

1 teaspoon low-carb sweetener of choice

Coconut oil or non-calorie cooking spray, for the pan

These pancakes are unusual in their inclusion of orange zest but don't let that stop you from trying them. They're sweet, creamy, and delicious, especially with some caramelized (or just freshly-sliced) thinly-sliced orange on top. Try them with vanilla protein ice cream on top, too, if you like!

MAKES 4 MEDIUM PANCAKES

1. Using a handheld immersion blender (or a small food processor), blend together all ingredients, except for the coconut oil, until you get a smooth batter.

2. Add a teaspoon of coconut oil or non-calorie cooking spray to a nonstick pan and heat the pan on high.

3. Pour your pancake batter on the pan and immediately turn down the heat to medium-low.

4. Flip the pancakes as soon as bubbles begin to form on the surface.

5. Repeat cooking steps for the rest of the batter.

6. Serve with your topping of choice.

Nutritional data for 4 pancakes: 404 kcals, 44 grams protein, 27 grams carbs, and 14 grams fat

PROTEIN MUG CAKES

Almond Butter Coffee
Mug Cake

Lemon Poppy Seed
Mug Cake

Cinnamon Peanut Butter
Mug Cake

Chocolate Mousse
Vegan Mug Cake

Almond Orange Mug
Cake

Carrot Mug Cake

Vegan Chocolate Protein
Mug Brownie

Mini Tiramisu Mug Cakes

Brownie Mug Cakes

Almond Vanilla Mug Cake

Dark Chocolate Protein
Mug Cake

Banana Mug Cake

Coconut and Pistachio
Mug Cake

Vegan Brownie Chocolate
Mud Mug Cake

It took me a while to come around to mug cakes, i.e., cakes in a mug cooked in the microwave. The first time I made them I was horribly disappointed! I had found a recipe online that involved just whey protein and eggs. There wasn't a picture involved but the author of the recipe claimed it was delicious, so I gave it a go. I vividly remember doing this before heading to the bus to meet my friend Ted, with whom I was going to see a movie. I was kind of hungry and figured I needed something filling and nice, so I opened my tub of whey, mixed it in with the egg in a mug, and stuck the whole thing in the microwave for two minutes. Those of you who have experience making protein mug cakes can probably guess what happened when I opened the microwave door: I was faced with something that can only be described as a thing. A shiny, tall, skinny-looking thing coming out of my mug. A firm believer in not judging a book by its cover, I grabbed a spoon and attempted to eat it. It didn't go well. The thing was as rubbery as the sole of a shoe and it tasted, oh . . . it tasted nasty. I left the house extremely disappointed—even Ted asked me what was wrong, to which I said nothing before quickly following it up with a summary of how a cake let me down. It took me years, literally, to make another mug cake. I just lost trust, you know? Bad recipes can do that to you.

Anyway, when I did try to make mug cakes again, I was equipped with something that I didn't have when I started out: the knowledge of how protein reacts when heated and an understanding of which ingredients need to be combined to ensure what you're making never disappoints. Here's what you need to know:

HEAT: Making a cake in the microwave is not the same as baking a cake in the oven. Think about the way in which a microwave cooks or heats up food: It does it from the middle outward. That's why you can sometimes heat up something, take it out of the microwave thinking it's warm enough, only to bite in and scald your mouth and injure your taste buds. To avoid this, take your mug cakes out of the microwave before they cook through completely and then let them sit for a bit before digging in. I include precise minute/second readings in each recipe. Please follow those and make sure you don't go over because, when it comes to mug cakes, every second counts!

MUGS: When making mug cakes, I suggest you consider using either a wide mug or a small (microwave-proof) ceramic bowl, as opposed to a tall and thin mug. That's because they will allow for your batter to cook more evenly. If you use a tall mug instead, the chances of over-cooking the center are much higher!

INGREDIENTS: If, by the end of this chapter, you feel that you have a good handle on mug cakes, enough to independently experiment with your own recipes, that's a mission accomplished from my end and I salute you. Just a quick reminder before you go on your first solo mission: Pay attention to your ingredients and make sure your batter is never more than one-third protein powder, especially when you're using whey. This will ensure you never end up with a monstrosity like the thing described above!

ALMOND BUTTER COFFEE MUG CAKE

I need to give you a warning about this cake: it's not the most beautiful thing in the world. Most mug cakes actually aren't—they're just cakes in a cup and when you take them out of the cup they look a bit, well . . . funny. But don't let their appearance deceive you into thinking mug cakes aren't tasty. They absolutely are! Take for example this one.

MAKES 1 CAKE

1. Using a handheld immersion blender (or a small food processor), blend together all ingredients, except for the dark chocolate, until you get a smooth paste.

2. Microwave in a mug for 45 seconds, wait 20 seconds, and then microwave for 30 seconds.

3. Insert a square of dark chocolate into your cake to create a chocolate filling or simply remove the cake from the mug, put it on a plate, and rub your chocolate on it to create a thin chocolate shell!

Nutritional data per cake: 307 kcals, 27 grams protein, 22 grams carbs, and 3 grams fat

½ tablespoon melted coconut oil

1 teaspoon baking powder

¼ cup whey protein powder

½ teaspoon stevia drops

3 tablespoons almond milk

1 teaspoon vanilla bean paste

1 tablespoon almond butter

½ tablespoon freshly brewed espresso

1 square (10 grams) dark chocolate

ADD SOME CHOPPED NUTS FOR A NICE CRUNCH.

LEMON POPPY SEED MUG CAKE

¼ cup whey protein powder

1 teaspoon baking powder

3 tablespoons almond milk

1 tablespoon granulated stevia (or your low-carb sweetener of choice)

1 tablespoon melted coconut oil

1 teaspoon vanilla bean paste

1 tablespoon ground almonds

½ teaspoon natural lemon flavoring

1 teaspoon poppy seeds

Ever since I first had a lemon poppy seed muffin, years and years ago now, I've loved the lemon and poppy seed combo. There's nothing quite like it, is there? Just like there's nothing quite like this mug cake. It's sweet and soft and, if you're into lemon poppy seed muffins, an absolute dream come true!

MAKES 1 CAKE

1. Using a handheld immersion blender (or a small food processor), blend together all ingredients until you get a smooth paste.

2. Microwave in a mug for 1 minute, wait 20 seconds, and then microwave for 20 seconds.

Nutritional data per cake: 224 kcals, 27 grams protein, 2 grams carbs, and 15 grams fat

CINNAMON PEANUT BUTTER MUG CAKE

This is the perfect accompaniment to a cup of tea or coffee! It's sweet and cakey and, if you want to turn it into more of a proper dessert, you can add a scoop of low-calorie or protein vanilla ice cream on top and then some sugar-free peanut butter sauce.

MAKES 1 CAKE

1. Using a handheld immersion blender (or a small food processor), blend together all ingredients until you get a smooth paste.

2. Microwave in a mug for 30 seconds, wait 5 seconds, microwave it for another 30 seconds, wait another 5 seconds, and then microwave for a final 30 seconds.

Nutritional data per cake: 385 kcals, 26 grams protein, 15 grams carbs, 24 grams fat

1 teaspoon cinnamon

1 large egg

2 tablespoons whey protein powder

4 tablespoons ground almonds

2 tablespoons almond milk

1 tablespoon smooth peanut butter

1 tablespoon agave syrup

1 teaspoon vanilla extract

CONSIDER TOPPING THE CAKE WITH MORE PEANUT BUTTER OR A SCOOP OF YOUR FAVORITE ICE CREAM TO TURN IT INTO MORE OF A DESSERT!

CHOCOLATE MOUSSE VEGAN MUG CAKE

2 tablespoons pea protein powder

3 tablespoons almond milk

½ tablespoon cocoa powder

2–3 pitted medjool dates, chopped

1 medium banana

½ tablespoon melted coconut oil

1 square (10 grams) dark chocolate (90%)

You may be wondering why I'm calling this cake a mousse cake. The answer is simple: Because it's creamy and really soft! Just like a mousse. Before I microwaved it, actually, I was tempted to just eat the batter. It's delicious!

MAKES 1 CAKE

1. Using a handheld immersion blender (or a small food processor), blend together all ingredients, except for the dark chocolate, until you get a smooth paste.

2. Microwave in a mug for 1 minute, wait 20 seconds, and then microwave for 30 seconds.

3. Insert a square of dark chocolate into your cake to create a chocolate filling.

Nutritional data per cake: 362 kcals, 14 grams protein, 58 grams carbs, and 9 grams fat

ALMOND ORANGE MUG CAKE

This cake is a tribute to my grandma, who used to add orange zest to all things almond and vanilla. It's a really nutty and sweet cake that's absolutely amazing with a scoop of a low-calorie or healthy vanilla protein ice cream on top. Especially if you add the ice cream right after you take the mug cake out of the microwave. Mm, mm, mmm!

MAKES 1 CAKE

Nutritional data per cake: 244 kcals, 17 grams protein, 14 grams carbs, and 9 grams fat

1. Using a handheld immersion blender (or a small food processor), blend together all ingredients until you get a smooth paste.

2. Microwave in a mug for 1 minute, wait 20 seconds, and then microwave for another minute.

¼ cup ground almonds

2 tablespoons pea protein powder

1 tablespoon coconut sugar

4 tablespoons almond milk

1 teaspoon cinnamon

1 tablespoon freshly grated orange zest

WANT TO UP THE PROTEIN IN THIS CAKE? SIMPLY ADD A SCOOP OF VANILLA PROTEIN ICE CREAM ON TOP AND/OR A TABLESPOON OF ALMOND BUTTER.

CARROT MUG CAKE

½ tablespoon cashew butter

¼ cup ground almonds

1 tablespoon agave or maple syrup

2 tablespoons almond or rice milk

2 tablespoons pea protein powder

½ teaspoon mixed spice

½ teaspoon cinnamon

½ teaspoon vanilla bean paste or vanilla extract

1 small grated carrot

Who doesn't love a good carrot cake, right? Especially if that carrot cake is made in under 5 minutes with only a few ingredients added in?

MAKES 1 CAKE

1. Using a handheld immersion blender (or a small food processor), blend together all the ingredients, except for the carrot, until you get a smooth paste.

2. Squeeze the grated carrot with a paper towel to remove any extra water from it. Mix the carrot into the batter.

3. Microwave in a mug for 1 minute, wait 20 seconds, and then microwave for 45 more seconds.

Nutritional data per cake: 194 kcals, 10 grams protein, 16 grams carbs, or 21 grams fat

CONSIDER TOPPING THIS CAKE WITH COCONUT CREAM, YOGURT, OR CREAM CHEESE!

VEGAN CHOCOLATE PROTEIN MUG BROWNIE

If you're one of those people who never bakes a batch of brownies because you end up eating them all, or at least far too many of them at once, this recipe is for you. It's single-serving, takes under five minutes, and requires just a few ingredients. Like the mug cakes before it, it's the perfect recipe to enjoy with a scoop of low-calorie, low-sugar, high-protein ice cream.

4 tablespoons canned chickpeas, drained

½ tablespoon cocoa powder

2 tablespoons pea protein powder

2 tablespoons coconut sugar

3 tablespoons almond milk

MAKES 1 BROWNIE

1. Using a handheld immersion blender (or a small food processor), blend together all ingredients until you get a smooth paste.

2. Microwave in a mug for 1 minute, wait 20 seconds, and then microwave for 30 to 45 seconds more.

Nutritional data per brownie: 211 kcals, 16 grams protein, 30 grams carbs, and 4 grams fat

TOP WITH FRUIT, DARK CHOCOLATE SAUCE, OR A SCOOP OF PROTEIN ICE CREAM!

MINI TIRAMISU MUG CAKES

Those of you who have a copy of my last book, *The Ultimate Protein Powder Cookbook*, know that protein tiramisu is a delicious food to make. It's just so easy! And it takes care of any/all cravings for proper Tiramisu—I think so at least. If you want to add some Tia Maria or another coffee liqueur to this recipe, by the way, to make this Tiramisu a bit boozy, go for it. Simply add a teaspoon or two to the cake and **POW!** you end up with tiramisu deliciousness.

MAKES 3 CAKES

1. Using a handheld immersion blender (or a small food processor), blend together all ingredients until you get a smooth paste.

2. Divide the batter into 3 small espresso cups and microwave them all together for 30 seconds.

3. Prepare your topping: Pour one tablespoon of coffee onto each cake and leave to cool.

4. Once cooled, mix the mascarpone with stevia and spoon on top of each cake.

5. Finish by sprinkling cocoa on top.

Nutritional data per cake: 132 kcals, 9 grams protein, 11 grams carbs, and 7 grams fat

Cake

4 tablespoons almond milk

1 tablespoon buckwheat flour

2 tablespoons coconut sugar

2 tablespoons pea protein powder

2 teaspoons instant coffee

2 tablespoons almond butter

1 teaspoon vanilla bean paste

Topping

3 tablespoons freshly brewed coffee

6 tablespoons low-fat mascarpone

1 tablespoon granulated stevia (or your low-carb sweetener of choice)

1 tablespoon cocoa powder

BROWNIE MUG CAKES

I've made this cake more times than I can remember. It's one of my favorites! You can probably tell by now that I'm really into chocolate—and this cake? Well, it delivers everything I want in a cake: sweetness, richness, and depth of flavor. I suggest you make this cake and let it sit overnight in the fridge before you eat it. It's absolutely delicious the day after!

½ cup canned black beans, drained

2 tablespoons cocoa powder

1 tablespoon pea protein powder

1 tablespoon agave, date syrup, or honey

3 pitted medjool dates

3 tablespoons almond milk

½–1 teaspoon stevia drops

2 tablespoons almond butter

1 square (10 grams) white chocolate (optional)

MAKES 2 CAKES

1. Using a handheld immersion blender (or a small food processor), blend together all ingredients, except for the white chocolate (if using), until you get a smooth paste.

2. Divide batter into two mugs and microwave each mug for 1 minute, wait 20 seconds, and then microwave for 10 to 20 seconds more.

3. Insert a square of white chocolate into your cake to create a chocolate filling.

Nutritional data per cake: 319 kcals, 16 grams protein, 39 grams carbs, and 11 grams fat

MAKE THIS BROWNIE CAKE TO USE AS THE FILING FOR THE CHOCOLATE BROWNIE CUPS ON PAGE 121!

ALMOND VANILLA MUG CAKE

This is a triple almond cake: It has ground almonds, almond milk, and almond extract! If you like almonds, you're in for a treat! It's perfect with some vanilla protein ice cream and some cinnamon on top and/or some orange zest.

MAKES 1 CAKE

1. Using a handheld immersion blender (or a small food processor), blend together all ingredients until you get a smooth paste.

2. Microwave in a mug for 30 seconds, wait 20 seconds, and microwave for 20 seconds more.

Nutritional data per cake: 334 kcals, 31 grams protein, 19 grams carbs, and 15 grams fat

2 tablespoons buckwheat flour

3 tablespoons almond milk

2 tablespoons whey protein powder

¼ cup ground almonds

½–1 teaspoon stevia drops

1 teaspoon natural almond extract

1 teaspoon vanilla bean paste

1 teaspoon melted coconut oil

DARK CHOCOLATE PROTEIN MUG CAKE

¼ cup whey protein powder

¼ cup almond milk

2 tablespoons cocoa powder

1 teaspoon low-carb sweetener of choice

2 tablespoons smooth peanut butter

1 teaspoon melted coconut oil

This cake is one of my go-to mug cakes to make on a weekend when I feel like having something sweet and decadent-tasting, but don't want to splurge on something sugary. It's really nice to eat with some low-calorie chocolate sauce or peanut butter on top!

MAKES 1 CAKE

1. Using a handheld immersion blender (or a small food processor), blend together all ingredients until you get a smooth paste.

2. Microwave in a mug for 30 seconds, wait 5 seconds, and then microwave for another 30 seconds.

3. Consider topping the cake with more peanut butter or a scoop of your favorite ice cream to turn it into more of a dessert!

Nutritional data per cake: 385 kcals, 34 grams protein, 14 grams carbs (4 grams of which are fiber!), and 25 grams fat

BANANA MUG CAKE

This mug cake is kind of like banana bread in a cup. You can actually add some walnuts to your batter, too, to make it even more banana-bready!

MAKES 1 CAKE

1. Using a handheld immersion blender (or a small food processor), blend together all ingredients until you get a smooth paste.

2. Microwave in a mug for 30 seconds, wait 20 seconds, and then microwave for 30 seconds more. If it's too mushy at that stage, microwave for another 30 seconds.

Nutritional data per cake: 314 kcals, 19 grams protein, 28 grams carbs, and 14 grams fat

1 medium banana

4 tablespoons ground almonds

2 tablespoons whey protein powder

1 tablespoon almond milk

1 teaspoon vanilla bean paste

½ teaspoon cinnamon

½ tablespoon buckwheat flour

CONSIDER TOPPING THIS CAKE WITH A SLICED BANANA, BANANA CHIPS, CHOCOLATE, AND/OR CHOPPED WALNUTS!

COCONUT AND PISTACHIO MUG CAKE

It took me a while to fall in love with coconut. I think it happened sometime in my twenties when, seemingly from one day to the next, I went from being lukewarm about coconut to absolutely loving it in any and all things. Nowadays, I add grated coconut to everything: to rice, chicken, salad (I know, weird), and cake. It's good in cake, I think, because it adds not only a great coconutty flavor, but it also makes the cake a bit crunchy and extra special. If you like pineapple or mango ice cream at all, it's a good one to enjoy with this cake!

¼ cup coconut flakes

2 tablespoons whey protein powder

2 tablespoons brown rice flour

1 teaspoon honey or agave syrup

2 teaspoons coconut oil

4 tablespoons almond or coconut milk

2 tablespoons pistachio nuts

MAKES 1 CAKE

1. Using a handheld immersion blender (or a small food processor), blend together all ingredients until you get a smooth paste.

2. Microwave for 30 seconds, wait 10 seconds, and then microwave for another 30 seconds.

Nutritional data per cake: 479 kcals, 17 grams protein, 43 grams carbs, and 28 grams fat

CONSIDER TOPPING THIS CAKE WITH COCONUT, CRANBERRIES, SUGAR-FREE ICE CREAM, NUTS, OR SOME SLICED BANANAS!

VEGAN BROWNIE CHOCOLATE MUD MUG CAKE

This cake is a cross between protein brownies and a traditional chocolate mud cake. It really tastes and feels like a chocolate mud cake. It's deeply chocolatey, soft, and rich. Unlike traditional chocolate mud cake, though, which is packed full of sugar and fat, this baby right here is under 400 calories and features a nice punch of protein that you can up by pairing the mug cake with some vanilla protein ice cream.

MAKES 1 CAKE

1. Using a handheld immersion blender (or a small food processor), blend together all ingredients until you get a smooth paste.

2. Microwave for 30 seconds, wait 10 seconds, microwave for another 30 seconds, wait 10 seconds, and microwave for another 30 seconds.

Nutritional data per cake: 383 kcals, 24 grams protein, 32 grams carbs, and 16 grams fat

⅓ cup canned chickpeas, drained

1 tablespoon almond butter

2 tablespoons pea protein powder

1 tablespoon date or agave syrup

1 tablespoon ground almonds

2 tablespoons almond milk

½ teaspoon stevia drops

1 tablespoon cocoa powder

CONSIDER TOPPING YOUR CAKE WITH SUGAR-FREE VANILLA ICE CREAM AND DARK CHOCOLATE FOR THE ULTIMATE MUG CAKE EXPERIENCE!

ACKNOWLEDGMENTS

I'd like to first thank my editor, Ann Treistman, without whom this book would have never happened. Thank you for your support, unmatched attention to detail, and believing in me and this book! As with our last book, *The Ultimate Protein Powder Cookbook*, this trailblazer of a book offers a totally new and original way of cooking—one where protein powder is used as an ingredient for making deliciously healthy snacks and meals. It takes a lot of daring and vision to publish these types of cookbooks because many people perceive protein powder as an overprocessed pseudo-food that no one (besides perhaps professional bodybuilders) really needs. But this book and our last one counter this thinking directly: by showing everyone firsthand that protein snacks are delicious, satisfying, nutrition-dense, and indeed natural. So thank you, Ann! Thank you for giving me the opportunity to introduce people across the world to cooking with protein powders and thinking outside the shake! Thank you for helping me spread the idea that protein powders aren't just a niche supplement, but a food ingredient that everyone can benefit from and use to make delicious healthy snacks.

I'd also like to thank my husband, whose constant love and support makes all my work possible. Thank you for always believing in me and encouraging me to chase my dreams, no matter how wild they are! And to our sweet little girl who, while of course not a vocal reviewer of this book, has many times contributed to my work by saying, "very nice Protein Pow recipes." Finally, thank you to my brother Chas, aka Tío Tito, and to my dad, who also doubles as my best friend. Love you all so much. You're my home and together, you're my people!

Last but not least, I'd like to thank the millions of people around the world who have tuned in to Protein Pow over the years. To those of you whom I've connected with on social media, and to those of you whom I've met personally through workshops and events, you make this journey such an awesome adventure! One of the biggest pleasures that's accompanied the building of Protein Pow is actually connecting with people like you—people around the world, who, like me, are passionate about nutrition, health, and great-tasting food. Together, we've created a style of cooking that has given rise to a community that transcends borders, languages, and backgrounds! So thank you for joining me; it's an honor to create and share this little world with you.

INDEX

Italicized pages refer to photos.

A

Almond(s), 67
banana mug cake, *186*, 187
and banana protein pancakes, *140*, *141*
carrot cake protein pancakes, 134, *135*
carrot mug cake, 176, *177*
chocolate orange bars, 60, *61*
cinnamon peanut butter mug cake, *170*, 171
cocoa nib coffee truffles, 96, 97
coffee protein truffles, 106, *107*
cranberry protein truffles, 98, 99
dark chocolate, protein truffles, 82, 83
dark chocolate, truffles, 76, 77
dark chocolate and, mania protein truffles, *100*, 101
lemon poppy seed mug cake, 168, *169*
orange mug cake, *174*, 175

orange sweet potato pancakes, 160, *161*
pecan dark chocolate bars, 50, *51*
protein coffee bars, *48*, 49
spinach protein pancakes, 130, *131*
vanilla mug cake, 183
vanilla orange oatmeal truffles, 94, 95
vegan, cranberry protein bars, 52, 53
vegan brownie chocolate mud mug cake, *190*, 191
vegan cashew bars, 62, 63

Almond butter
apple pie bars, 40, 41
brownie mug cakes, 182, *183*
chocolate orange bars, 60, *61*
coffee mug cake, 166, 167
dark chocolate almond truffles, 76, 77
dark chocolate and almond mania protein truffles, *100*, 101

Almond butter (*continued*)

    honey and whey protein bars, *44*, 45

    mini tiramisu mug cakes, *180*, 181

    orange vanilla protein cups, *112*, 113

    protein coffee bars, *48*, 49

    strawberry shortcake whey truffles, *70*, 71

    vanilla orange oatmeal truffles, *94*, 95

    vegan almond cranberry protein bars, *52*, 53

    vegan chocolate protein bars, 36, 37

Amino acids, 13

Apple(s)

    pie bars, *40*, 41

    and white chocolate protein pancakes, 145

Apricots: spice and all things nice truffles, 92, 93

B

Baby formulas, 18

    whey protein powder in, 18-19

Bananas

    almond and, protein pancakes, *140*, 141

    chocolate mousse vegan mug cake, *172*, *173*

    chocolate protein pancakes, *132*, 133

    dairy-free protein pancakes, *158*, 159

    mug cake, *186*, 187

    nut protein pancakes, *136*, 137

    spinach protein pancakes, *130*, *131*

    vegan, pancakes, 152, *153*

    whey protein pancakes, 126, *127*

Black beans

    brownie mug cakes, 182

    chocolate brownie cups, *120*, *121*

Blenders, 28

    immersion, 28

Blueberries

    cranberry and, protein pancakes, *142*, *143*

    vegan banana pancakes, 152, *153*

Brazil nuts, 67

    macadamia energy truffles, 88, *89*

Buttermilk Protein Pancakes, *128*, 129

Butternut Squash Protein Pancakes, 138, *139*

C

Cantaloupe: melon pancakes, 144

Carrots

    cake protein pancakes, 134, *135*

    mug cake, 176, *177*

Cashew(s)

    vegan, bars, 62, 63

    white chocolate and lemon zest protein truffles, 80, *81*

Cashew butter

    carrot mug cake, 176, *177*

    chocolate chip cookie dough truffles, 68, 69

    chocolate orange bars, 60, *61*

    mini white chocolate goji cups, 116, *117*

    nut seed honey goji bars, 64, 65

    vegan, bars, 62, 63

    vegan cashew bars, 62, 63

    vegan chocolate chip cookie dough bars, 38, 39

    vegan hemp matcha, 33-34, 35

Chickpeas

    vegan brownie chocolate mud mug cake, 190, 191

    vegan chocolate protein mug brownie, *178*, 179

Chocolate. *See also* Dark chocolate; White
    chocolate
    brownie cups, *120,* 121
    coconut energy truffles, 90, *91*
    mousse vegan mug cake, 172, *173*
    orange bars, 60, *61*
    protein pancakes, *132,* 133
    protein powder, 18
Chocolate chips: cookie dough truffles, *68,*
    69
Cinnamon Peanut Butter Mug Cake, *170,*
    171
Cocoa/cocoa powder, 17–18
    brownie mug cakes, 182
    chocolate brownie cups, *120,* 121
    chocolate coconut energy truffles, 90, *91*
    chocolate mousse vegan mug cake, 172,
        173
    chocolate protein pancakes, *132,* 133
    cocoa nib coffee truffles, 96, 97
    coffee protein truffles, 106, *107*
    dark chocolate almond truffles, 76, *77*
    dark chocolate and almond mania protein
        truffles, *100,* 101
    dark chocolate goji truffles, *78,* 79
    dark chocolate protein mug cake, 184, *185*
    double chocolate bars, 42, *43*
    double chocolate protein cups, 114, *115*
    hemp, dark chocolate truffles, 102, *103*
    hemp protein bars, 57–58, *59*
    mini tiramisu mug cakes, *180,* 181
    peanut dark chocolate bars, 54, *55*
    vegan, pow truffles, *86,* 87
    vegan brownie chocolate mud mug cake,
        190, 191

vegan chocolate protein bars, 36, 37
vegan double-chocolate protein truffles,
    82, 83
Cocoa Nib Coffee Truffles, 96, 97
Coconut
    chocolate, energy truffles, 90, *91*
    matcha and, protein truffles, 84, *85*
    mini white chocolate goji cups, *116,* 117
    and pistachio mug cake, *188,* 189
    and whey protein bars, 46, *47*
Coffee. *See also* espresso
    double chocolate protein cups, 114, *115*
    mini tiramisu mug cakes, *180,* 181
    protein, bar, 48, *49*
    protein truffles, 106, *107*
Cranberries
    almond, protein truffles, 98, 99
    and blueberry protein pancakes, *142,*
        143
    spice and all things nice truffles, 92, 93
    vegan almond, protein bars, 52, 53
Cupboard ingredients, 26–27

D
Dairy-Free Protein Pancakes, *158,* 159
Dark chocolate
    almond butter coffee mug cake, *166,* 167
    and almond mania protein truffles, *100,*
        101
    almond protein truffles, *82,* 83
    almond truffles, 76, *77*
    brownie cups, *120,* 121
    chocolate brownie cups, *120,* 121
    chocolate chip cookie dough truffles, 68,
        69

Dark chocolate (*continued*)

  chocolate mousse vegan mug cake, 172, *173*

  chocolate orange bars, 60, *61*

  cocoa nib coffee truffles, 96, 97

  coconut and whey protein bars, 46, *47*

  coffee protein truffles, 106, *107*

  double, bars, 42, *43*

  double, protein cups, 114, *115*

  goji truffles, *78*, 79

  hemp cocoa, truffles, 102, *103*

  hemp protein bars, 57-58, *59*

  honey and whey protein bars, *44*, 45

  matcha and coconut protein truffles, 84, *85*

  mini peanut butter protein cups, *110*, 111

  mousse vegan mug cake, 172, *173*

  nut seed honey goji bars, 64, 65

  orange bars, 60, *61*

  orange vanilla protein cups, *112*, 113

  peanut, bars, 54, *55*, 56

  peanut butter and, chocolate protein truffles, *74*, 75

  pecan, bars, 50, *51*

  protein coffee bars, *48*, 49

  protein mug cake, 184, *185*

  sunflower honey protein cups, 118, *119*

  sunflower honey protein truffles, *104*, 105

  vanilla orange oatmeal truffles, *94*, 95

  vegan, cookie dough bars, 38, 39

  vegan almond cranberry protein bars, 52, 53

  vegan cashew bars, 62, 63

  vegan chocolate chip cookie dough bars, 38, *39*

  vegan cocoa pow truffles, *86, 87*
Dates

  almond cranberry protein truffles, 98, 99

  brownie mug cakes, 182

  chocolate brownie cups, *120*, 121

  chocolate mousse vegan mug cake, 172, *173*

  cranberry and blueberry protein pancakes, *142*, 143

  macadamia energy truffles, 88, 89

  maple and flax protein pancakes, 156, *157*

  protein coffee bars, *48*, 49

  spice and all things nice truffles, 92, 93

  vegan hemp matcha potein bars, 35, 36
Double Chocolate Bars, 42, *43*
Double Chocolate Protein Cups, 114, *115*
Duration, 29

E

Equipment, 28
Espresso. *See also* Coffee

  almond butter coffee mug cake, *166*, 167

  chocolate coconut energy truffles, 90, *91*

  cocoa nib coffee truffles, 96, 97

  protein coffee bars, 49, 50

F

Figs: almond cranberry protein truffles, 98, 99
Flaxseed

  maple and, protein pancakes, 156, *157*

  protein pancakes, 148, *149*
Fridge ingredients, 27

G

Gloves, 29

Goji berries

dark chocolate, truffles, *78, 79*

mini white chocolate, cups, *116,* 117

nut seed honey, bars, 64, *65*

Guar gum, 17

H

Hazelnuts: vegan chocolate protein bars, 37, *38*

Hemp Cocoa Dark Chocolate Truffles, 102, *103*

Hemp protein, 17, 20, 21

bars, 57–58, *59*

cocoa dark chocolate truffles, 102, *103*

vegan hemp matcha protein bars, 33–34, 35

Hemp Protein Bars, 57–58, *59*

Hemp seeds

dark chocolate goji truffles, *78, 79*

hemp cocoa dark chocolate truffles, 102, *103*

spice and all things nice truffles, *92,* 93

Honey

spice and all things nice truffles, *92,* 93

sunflower, protein truffles, *104,* 105

and whey protein bars, *44,* 45

I

Immersion blender, 28

Ingredients

cupboard, 26–27

fridge, 27

L

Lemon Poppy Seed Mug Cake, 168, *169*

Lemon zest: white chocolate and, protein truffles, 80, *81*

M

Macadamia nuts

energy truffles, 88, *89*

protein pancakes, *150,* 151

Macronutrients, 14

Maple and Flax Protein Pancakes, 156, *157*

Mascarpone: mini tiramisu mug cakes, *180,* 181

Matcha

and coconut protein truffles, 84, *85*

vegan hemp, protein bars, 33–34, 35

Measurements, 25–27

Melon pancakes, 144

Micronutrients, 14

Mini Peanut Butter Protein Cups, *110,* 111

Mini Tiramisu Mug Cakes, *180,* 181

Mini White Chocolate Goji Cups, *116,* 117

Mugs, 164

N

Nut butters, 28. *See also* Almond butter; Cashew butter

Nut Seed Honey Goji Bars, 64, *65*

O

Oats

almond cranberry protein truffles, 98, *99*

apple and white chocolate protein pancakes, 145

Oats (*continued*)

    buttermilk protein pancakes, *128,* 129

    carrot cake protein pancakes, 134, *135*

    chocolate coconut energy truffles, 90, *91*

    cranberry and blueberry protein pan-
        cakes, *142, 143*

    dairy-free protein pancakes, *158,* 159

    macadamia nut pancakes, *150,* 151

    maple and flax protein pancakes, 156, *157*

    melon pancakes, 144

    spinach protein pancakes, 130, *131*

    strawberry shortcake whey truffles, 70, *71*

    sweet potato pancakes, *124, 125*

    vanilla orange oatmeal truffles, 94, *95*

    vegan banana pancakes, 152, *153*

    vegan hemp matcha protein bars, 33–34, *35*

Orange zest

    almond, mug cake, 174, *175*

    chocolate orange bars, 60, *61*

    sweet potato protein pancakes, 160, *161*

    vanilla orange oatmeal truffles, 94, *95*

    vanilla protein cups, *112,* 113

P

Peanut butter

    and chocolate protein truffles, *74,* 75

    cinnamon, mug cake, 170, *171*

    dairy-free protein pancakes, *158,* 159

    dark chocolate protein mug cake, 184, *185*

    double chocolate bars, 42, *43*

    and jelly truffles, 72, *73*

    mini, protein cups, *110,* 111

    vegan banana pancakes, 152, *153*

    vegan chocolate chip cookie dough bars,
        38, *39*

Peanut Dark Chocolate Bars, 54, 55, 56

Pea protein, 17, 20, 21

    almond orange mug cake, 174, *175*

    apple pie bars, 40, *41*

    banana nut protein pancakes, 136, *137*

    brownie mug cakes, 182

    buttermilk protein pancakes, *128,* 129

    carrot mug cake, 176, *177*

    chocolate brownie cups, *120,* 121

    chocolate mousse vegan mug cake, 172, *173*

    coffee protein truffles, 106, *107*

    dairy-free protein pancakes, *158,* 159

    dark chocolate goji truffles, 78, *79*

    double chocolate protein cups, 114, *115*

    flaxseed protein pancakes, 148, *149*

    macadamia energy truffles, 88, *89*

    macadamia nut pancakes, *150,* 151

    mini tiramisu mug cakes, *180,* 181

    nut seed honey goji bars, 64, *65*

    orange sweet potato pancakes, 160, *161*

    spice and all things nice truffles, 92, *93*

    sunflower honey protein cups, 118, *119*

    sunflower honey protein truffles, *104,* 105

    vanilla orange oatmeal truffles, 94, 94, *95*

    vegan almond cranberry protein bars, 52,
        53

    vegan banana pancakes, 152, *153*

    vegan brownie chocolate mud mug cake,
        190, 191

    vegan cashew bars, 62, *63*

    vegan chocolate chip cookie dough bars,
        38, *39*

    vegan chocolate protein bars, 36, *37*

    vegan chocolate protein mug brownie,
        178, 179

vegan cocoa pow truffles, *86, 87*

vegan crepe-style pancakes, *154, 155*

vegan double-chocolate protein truffles, *82, 83*

Pecan Dark Chocolate Bars, 50, *51*

Pistachio nuts

    coconut and pistachio mug cake, 189

    coffee protein truffles, 106, *107*

Plant-based protein powders, 10

Poppy seeds: lemon, mug cake, 168, *169*

Protein(s)

    as key nutrient, 13–14

    requirements of, 14

    single-ingredient, 17

Protein bars, 30–65

    apple pie, *40, 41*

    chocolate orange, 60, *61*

    coconut and whey, 46, *47*

    coffee, *48, 49*

    convenience of, 31–32

    double chocolate, 42, *43*

    hemp, 57–58, *59*

    honey and whey, *44, 45*

    nut seed honey goji, 64, *65*

    peanut dark chocolate, 54, *55*, 56

    pecan dark chocolate, 50, *51*

    vegan almond cranberry, *52*, 53

    vegan cashew, 62, *63*

    vegan chocolate, 36, *37*

    vegan chocolate chip cookie dough, 38, *39*

    vegan hemp matcha, 33–34, *35*

Protein chocolate cups, 108–121

    brownie, *120*, 121

    double, 114, *115*

    mini peanut butter, *110*, 111

    mini white, goji cups, *116*, 117

    orange vanilla, *112, 113*

    sunflower honey, 118, *119*

Protein mug cakes, 162–191

    almond butter coffee, *166, 167*

    almond orange, *174, 175*

    almond vanilla, 183

    banana, *186*, 187

    brownie, 182

    carrot, 176, *177*

    chocolate mousse vegan, 172, *173*

    cinnamon peanut butter, *170*, 171

    coconut, *188*, 189

    dark chocolate, 184, *185*

    lemon poppy seed, 168, *169*

    mini tiramisu, *180, 181*

    vegan brownie chocolate, *190, 191*

    vegan chocolate, brownie, *178, 179*

Protein pancakes, 122–161

    almond and banana, *140, 141*

    apple and white chocolate, 145

    banana nut, *136, 137*

    banana whey, 126, *127*

    buttermilk, *128*, 129

    butternut squash, 138, *139*

    carrot cake, 134, *135*

    chocolate protein, *132, 133*

    cranberry and blueberry, *142, 143*

    dairy-free, *158, 159*

    flaxseed, 148, *149*

    macadamia nut, *150*, 151

    maple and flax, 156, *157*

    melon, 144

    orange sweet potato, 160, *161*

    ricotta whey, *146, 147*

Protein pancakes (*continued*)

    spinach, 130, *131*

    sweet potato, *124, 125*

    vegan banana, 152, *153*

    vegan crepe-style, *154*, 155

Protein powders, 15–22

    buying, 24–25

    "chocolate," 18

    choosing, 17–18

    knowing your, 25

    as mainstream, 11

    making, 18–20

    marketing of, 16–17

    measurements and, 25–27

    plant-based, 10

    as pseudo-food, 10

    shopping guide for, 24–25

    sustainability and, 21

    for women, 21–22

Protein shakes, 9

Protein snacks, reasons for making own, 23–24

Protein truffles, 66–107

    almond cranberry, 98, 99

    chocolate chip cookie dough, *68*, 69

    chocolate coconut energy, 90, *91*

    cocoa nib coffee, 96, 97

    coffee, 106, *107*

    dark chocolate almond, 76, *77*, *82*, 83

    dark chocolate and almond mania, *100*, 101

    dark chocolate goji, *78*, 79

    hemp cocoa dark chocolate, 102, *103*

    macadamia energy, 88, 89

    matcha and coconut, 84, *85*

    peanut butter and chocolate, *74*, 75

    peanut butter and jelly, 72, 73

    spice and all things nice, *92*, 93

    strawberry shortcake whey, 70, 71

    sunflower honey, *104*, 105

    vanilla orange oatmeal, 94, 95

    vegan cocoa pow, 86, 87

    white chocolate and lemon zest, 80, 81

Pumpkin seeds

    nut seed honey goji bars, 64, 65

    spice and all things nice truffles, 92, 93

R

Raisins: spice and all things nice truffles, 92, 93

Rice protein, 20, 21

Ricotta Whey Protein Pancakes, *146*, 147

S

Servings, size of, in recipes, 28

Shopping guide for buying protein powders, 24–25

Single-ingredient proteins, 17

Spice and All things Nice Truffles, 92, 93

Spinach Protein Pancakes, 130, *131*

Storage, 29

Strawberries

    peanut butter and jelly truffles, 72, 73

    shortcake whey truffles, 70, 71

Sunflower butter

    honey, protein truffles, *104*, 105

    sunflower honey protein cups, 118, *119*

Sunflower seeds, 67

    dark chocolate goji truffles, *78*, 79

Sustainability, protein powders and, 21

Sweet potato
  orange, pancakes, 160, *161*
  pancakes, *124, 125*

U

The Ultimate Protein Powder Cookbook, 11,
  181, 193

V

Vanilla Orange Oatmeal Truffles, 94, *95*
Vegan Almond Cranberry Protein Bars, *52,*
  53
Vegan Banana Protein Pancakes, 152, *153*
Vegan Brownie Chocolate Mud Mug Cake,
  190, 191
Vegan Cashew Bars, 62, *63*
Vegan Chocolate Chip Cookie Dough Bars,
  38, *39*
Vegan Chocolate Protein Bars, 36, *37*
Vegan Chocolate Protein Mug Brownie, *178,*
  179
Vegan Cocoa Pow Truffles, 86, *87*
Vegan Crepe-Style Protein Pancakes, *154,*
  155
Vegan Hemp Matcha Protein Bars, 33–34,
  35
Veggie protein powders, 20

W

Walnuts
  banana nut protein pancakes, 136, *137*
  carrot cake protein pancakes, 134, *135*
  spice and all things nice truffles, *92,*
    93
Whey, 21

Whey protein, 10–11, 17, 18–20
  almond and banana protein pancakes,
    140, 141
  almond butter coffee mug cake, *166, 167*
  almond cranberry protein truffles, 98, *99*
  almond vanilla mug cake, 183
  apple and white chocolate protein pan-
    cakes, 145
  in baby formulas, 18–19
  banana, pancakes, 126, *127*
  banana mug cake, *186,* 187
  buttermilk protein pancakes, *128, 129*
  butternut squash pancakes, 138, *139*
  carrot cake protein pancakes, 134, *135*
  chocolate chip cookie dough truffles, 68,
    69
  chocolate coconut energy truffles, 90, *91*
  chocolate orange bars, 60, *61*
  cinnamon peanut butter mug cake, *170,*
    171
  chocolate protein pancakes, *132,* 133
  cocoa nib coffee truffles, 96, *97*
  coconut and whey protein bars, 46, *47*
  coconut and pistachio mug cake, *188, 189*
  cranberry and blueberry protein pan-
    cakes, *142,* 143
  dark chocolate almond truffles, 76, *77*
  dark chocolate and almond mania protein
    truffles, *100,* 101
  dark chocolate protein mug cake, 184, *185*
  double chocolate bars, 42, *43*
  honey and whey protein bars, *44,* 45
  lemon poppy seed mug cake, 168, *169*
  maple and flax protein pancakes, 156, *157*
  matcha and coconut protein truffles, 84, *85*

Whey protein (*continued*)

melon pancakes, 144

mini peanut butter protein cups, *110, 111*

mini white chocolate goji cups, *116, 117*

orange sweet potato pancakes, 160, *161*

orange vanilla protein cups, *112,* 113

peanut butter and chocolate, truffles, *74, 75*

peanut butter and jelly truffles, 72, *73*

peanut dark chocolate bars, 54, 55, 56

pecan dark chocolate bars, 50, *51*

protein coffee bars, 49, 50

ricotta, pancakes, *146, 147*

spinach protein pancakes, 130, *131*

strawberry shortcake, truffles, 70, 71

sweet potato pancakes, *124,* 125

white chocolate and lemon zest protein truffles, 80, *81*

White chocolate

apple and, protein pancakes, 145

brownie mug cakes, 182

chocolate brownie cups, *120,* 121

cocoa nib coffee truffles, 96, 97

and lemon zest protein truffles, 80, *81*

mini, goji cups, 116, *116,* 117, *117*

nut seed honey goji bars, 64, 65

Women, protein powders for, 21–22

X

Xanthan gum, 17